Grilling Basics
FOR
DUMMIES®

by John Mariani, Marie Rama,
Tere Drenth, and Lucy Wing

WILEY

Wiley Publishing, Inc.

Grilling Basics For Dummies®

Published by
Wiley Publishing, Inc.
111 River St.
Hoboken, NJ 07030-5774
www.wiley.com

WILEY

About the Authors

John Mariani is the author of several of the most highly regarded books on food in America today, including *The Dictionary of American Food & Drink* and *The Dictionary of Italian Food & Drink*. He is currently food and travel correspondent for *Esquire;* Food, Wine, Beer & Spirits Board Expert for PRODIGY interactive service, for which he also produces the weekly *Mariani's Virtual Gourmet Newsletter;* dining columnist for *Wine Spectator;* food columnist for *Diversion;* columnist for *Eating Well;* Food & Drink columnist for *Sports Afield;* and columnist for *Restaurant Hospitality.*

Marie Rama is coauthor of *Cooking For Dummies.* She has worked as a professional pastry chef and recipe developer for numerous food companies and associations, including The McIlhenny Company and The United Fresh Fruit and Vegetable Association. Marie served as Director of Romance, Weddings, and Entertainment for Korbel Champagne and as a spokesperson for Sunkist Growers. She is a regular guest-chef on hundreds of TV and radio shows in the U.S. and Canada.

Tere Drenth, a freelance writer and editor, has edited numerous cookbooks, including *Grilling For Dummies* and *Seafood Cooking For Dummies,* which earned the "Best Cookbook on Fish" award at the Versailles World Cookbook Fair. She co-authored *Indoor Grilling For Dummies.*

Lucy Wing, former Executive Food Editor at *Country Living* magazine and Food Editor at *McCall's,* grills as part of her everyday cooking and entertaining lifestyle. She often dishes up both outdoor and indoor grilled foods in the same meal and has been known to grill even with snow piled high around the area. Whether grilling on her rooftop in New York City, at her farmhouse in Pennsylvania, or on the patio in Arizona, only high winds force her to cease grilling outdoors to retreat to full-time indoor grilling. Passionate not only about grilling, Lucy maintains gardens where she resides and often uses the bounty of her vegetables, fruits, flowers, and herbs in her recipes and food articles.

Publisher's Acknowledgments

We're proud of this book; please send us your comments through our Dummies online registration form located at www.dummies.com/register/. For information about a custom Dummies book for your business or organization, contact BrandedRights&Licenses@Wiley.com.

Some of the people who helped bring this book to market include the following:

Acquisitions, Editorial, and Media Development

Senior Project Editor: Zoë Wykes

Business Development Representative: Karen L. Hattan

Editorial Manager: Rev Mengle

Cover Photo: The Companion Group

Cartoon: Rich Tennant
(www.the5thwave.com)

Composition Services

Project Coordinator: Kristie Rees

Layout and Graphics: Lauren Goddard, Jacque Roth, Julie Trippetti

Special Art: Elizabeth Kurtzman

Proofreader: Laura Albert, Jessica Kramer, Christine Pingleton, Dwight Ramsey

Indexer: Johnna VanHoose

Special Help: Gabriele McCann

Publishing and Editorial for Consumer Dummies

    Diane Graves Steele, Vice President and Publisher, Consumer Dummies

    Joyce Pepple, Acquisitions Director, Consumer Dummies

    Kristin A. Cocks, Product Development Director, Consumer Dummies

    Michael Spring, Vice President and Publisher, Travel

    Kelly Regan, Editorial Director, Travel

Publishing for Technology Dummies

    Andy Cummings, Vice President and Publisher, Dummies Technology/General User

Composition Services

    Gerry Fahey, Vice President of Production Services

    Debbie Stailey, Director of Composition Services

Table of Contents

The 5th Wave

By Rich Tennant

©RICHTENNANT

"I'm pretty sure it's grilled game. That would explain the meat tasting like a Monopoly game board."

Introduction

*W*elcome to *Grilling Basics For Dummies!* This book takes you through the basics of grilling and then shows you the infinite possibilities of this terrific cooking technique. Even if you've done a certain amount of serious grilling, this book can help you to refine your technique. The book also introduces you to many foods you may never even have considered suitable for grilling, including vegetables and fruits.

Plus, we try very hard to take the intimidation factor out of the process and replace it with a whole lot of fun.

About This Book

Grilling Basics For Dummies is a book that will make an expert grill master out of you — or at least make the exercise painless. But it's not just a book of recipes or tips on how to care for a grill. The recipes and tips are all in here, but the book includes a great deal more.

Grilling has its own jargon and requires its own accessories, so we explain grilling jargon and tell you what accessories you need. When you get to the recipe chapters, you find that we discuss the kinds of food that are great on the grill and how to select them. The recipes range from classic to contemporary — all perfect for the grill. We even give you some quick information on ways to make grilling healthy and safe.

You need not read the book straight through. In fact, we've deliberately arranged it for those who already know a bit about grilling as well as for those who are just beginners. So go right ahead: Read the book in any order you want. That's why this book looks and reads the way it does.

How This Book Is Organized

As with all *For Dummies* books, *Grilling Basics For Dummies* is arranged for maximum ease of use. We break down subjects into simple-to-understand chapters, within which we cover specific subjects and topics, often with lists for handy reference.

In the first three chapters, we get you up to speed on what all those grilling terms mean and even provide a checklist of grilling accessories! We also help you stock your pantry with the kinds of foods and seasonings that make for great grilling. Anyone can slap down a sirloin on a grill, but this part suggests rubs, sauces, and marinades that can add flavor and texture to your grilled foods.

Then, in Chapters 4 through 8, we cover old-fashioned favorites like burgers (there's more to a great burger than buying a frozen patty at the supermarket, you know), hot dogs, and kebabs. We also take you beyond the old-fashioned grilled foods and invite you to try a variety of steak, pork, and chicken recipes. We even give you tips about how to buy the best cut for your purposes.

And if you thought grilling involved only meat and poultry, we show you that the grill is one of the most versatile cooking methods imaginable for adding taste to seafood (Chapter 7) and vegetables (Chapter 8). And if you've never considered making sandwiches on the grill, we think that you'll be surprised by the possibilities (Chapter 8).

In the back of the book, we give you ten (actually nine) tips for grilling the safe and healthy way.

Icons Used in This Book

We fill our book with icons that alert you to something you may not have thought of but that will help make outdoor cooking a lot more pleasurable. Here's what the icons mean:

This icon gives you tips on the best meats, seafood, vegetables, seasonings, and equipment.

These tips give helpful information about successful grilling techniques for individual foods, from temperature control to ease of cleanup.

Sometimes you just need to hear something again. This icon serves as a reminder of some advice that we offer elsewhere in the book. These are also helpful hints to keep in mind after you put this book down!

All cooking involves a certain degree of danger, and safety should always be on the mind of anyone doing any grilling. This icon reminds you of ways to avoid personal injury or property damage.

In addition, we offer two ways to stretch the recipes in this book:

Vary It! When you're grilling, there's never just one way to prepare a recipe. So, we highlight ways that you can improvise and give you ideas for varying the preparation or the ingredients.

Go-With! These give you ideas for side dishes to pair with tasty grilled main dishes, marinades and sauces that work well with your chosen meat, and grilled fruits and breads that go with delicious recipes throughout the book.

A Few Guidelines Before You Begin

Every cook has his or her preferences, so it's best to know ours before you begin sampling our recipes. Here are some guidelines:

> ✔ All recipe cooking times are just estimates. The temperature of the air and the food and the intensity of the grill's heat can affect, sometimes radically, the amount of time needed to grill food. Our best advice is to experiment with your own grill and adjust the cooking times of our recipes accordingly.

✔ Most recipes call for temperatures like "medium," "medium-low," or "high" because most grills don't have temperature gauges. When temperatures are mentioned, however, they're in degrees Fahrenheit.

✔ Marinate all foods in the refrigerator in non-metal or non-reactive containers like glass or ceramic. Plastic, resealable bags are excellent for this purpose and take up less space than dishes. (Flip to Chapter 3 for more on marinating.)

✔ Never use leftover marinade as a finishing sauce unless you thoroughly boil the marinade to kill any possible bacteria picked up from the raw food.

✔ Although some cookbooks may say to bring your food to room temperature before cooking, with few exceptions, we don't recommend this tip for grilled foods. If the temperature is in the 80s or 90s, foods can spoil quickly.

✔ Salt can add tremendous flavor and even a little texture to grilled food. The optimum time to salt food is just before you place it on the grill. You can add more salt and sprinkle on the pepper (which should always be freshly ground) after you remove the food from the grill.

✔ Before firing up your grill, brush the grill grid with a vegetable oil, such as peanut or corn oil. (Some grillers find it easier to use a nonstick cooking spray.) This step helps to keep the food from sticking unpleasantly to the grill grid. Never brush or spray the grid while the grill is hot, because this can cause dangerous flare-ups.

✔ Always read all safety information and every warning icon (like this one) in this book. Following the safety advice is absolutely essential if you want to have a pleasant grilling experience.

Chapter 1

Mastering Grill-Speak

● ●

● ●

*N*othing — not roasting, not frying, not sautéing, and certainly not poaching — gives such wonderful, smoky flavor to food as grilling does. And because it's done outdoors, grilling is the most social of cooking techniques. For as long as people have known how great foods can taste when cooked over an open fire, grilling has been a social event that invites people to participate. Grilling often gathers friends, neighbors, and family members around the grill to share stories, trade recipes, and even help cook.

In this chapter, we start off with some translation for you — from Grill-Speak into everyday language.

Two Key Terms: Direct Grilling and Indirect Grilling

In your introduction to the language of grilling, we start you off with the two basic methods of grilling — direct and indirect.

Direct — no-frills grilling

Direct grilling means that the food is placed on the grill directly over the full force of the heat source, whether it's electric, charcoal, hardwood, or gas. Just about every food, from meats to vegetables, can be grilled directly. Some foods, however, are better cooked over indirect heat, a great grilling technique that's introduced in the following section. Foods that are often grilled directly over the heat include hamburgers, hot dogs, pork chops, boneless chicken breasts, steaks, and all types of fish and shellfish.

Grilling over direct, intense heat sears the food, coating its exterior with a tasty brown crust that's loaded with flavor. Direct grilling, the focus of this book, is a fast cooking technique that doesn't require elaborate finishing sauces. Simple marinades, salsas, and condiments (all covered in Chapter 3) are all you need to complement directly grilled meat.

The primary difficulty with direct grilling is that you must watch your food closely to prevent it from burning.

Indirect — pushing food away from the heat

Indirect grilling grills foods slowly, off to one side of the heat source, usually over a *drip pan* (a pan that catches dripping fat from grilled food) in a covered grill. If you want to use this technique with a charcoal or gas grill, here's what you do:

- ✔ Place the food on the grill grid so that it's away from or to the side of the full force of the heat. In a gas grill with two burners, you ignite only one burner and place the food over the unlit burner. If your gas grill has only one burner, place the food in an aluminum foil pan or on several layers of foil and grill over very low heat. Always preheat your gas grill with all burners on high and the lid down for about 15 minutes; then turn one of the burners off before cooking indirectly. In a charcoal grill, arrange the lit coals around the drip pan or bank them to one side of the pan.

- ✔ Whether you're using a gas or charcoal grill, place a drip pan directly under the food. You can fill the pan with water or another liquid, such as broth or apple juice, to add moisture and keep the slow-cooking food from drying out.

> ✔ Close the grill lid to cover the grill, trap the heat and smoke, and mimic the desirable effects of slow, oven roasting.
>
> ✔ To collect pan juices (especially with large roasts), place the food in a roasting pan and then set the pan on the grill.

Indirectly grill any large cuts of meat or whole birds, pork tenderloins, ribs, or large roasts for delicious results.

Another Term to Know: Barbecuing

Barbecuing is the technique of indirectly and slowly cooking large cuts of meat for a long period of time, over low heat and with lots of hot smoke. Compare this to direct grilling, which cooks small, tender pieces of food at higher temperatures for shorter grilling times. You might say that the two techniques are almost opposites.

Barbecuing generally takes tough cuts of meat and cooks or breaks down connective tissue into tender morsels that practically fall apart. Foods that are barbecued often include beef brisket, whole hogs, pork shoulder, and pork ribs. These foods are perfect for barbecuing because they actually *demand* to be cooked for long periods to break down their stubborn tissues and release flavor.

More Vocabulary: Smoking

The technique of *smoking* food differs from barbecuing because it uses even lower heat to slow down the cooking process. Food cooks for hours, and becomes infused with hot, aromatic smoke. The cooking temperatures for smoking foods range from 180 degrees to 250 degrees. You can choose from two methods — dry or wet — and both can be duplicated on your kettle grill. However, if you do use your kettle grill, you should place a temperature gauge on the grill to monitor and keep the heat within the proper temperature range. A 7-pound whole turkey or a 12- to 14-pound ham can take 9 hours or more to smoke. A 5- to 7-pound roast beef takes 5 to 6 hours to reach an internal temperature of 140 degrees. At many professional barbecue eateries and stores, beef and pork are smoked for 12 hours or more at a very low heat.

And the Rest of the Terms: A Griller's Glossary

To help you wade through the Grill-Speak that you may hear when shopping for grills and accessories — or from your neighbor down the street — we compiled the following glossary of terms. Use these, and you'll be a grilling guru in no time.

- **Baste:** To brush a seasoned liquid over the surface of food to add moisture and flavor.

- **Brazier:** An inexpensive, open charcoal grill with a grill grid that is usually just a few inches from the coals. Best for quick grilling.

- **Ceramic briquettes:** These briquettes are made of radiant materials and are used in gas grills to transfer heat from the burners and spread it evenly under the grill grid. Briquettes made of ceramic don't burn up like charcoal briquettes do. *Lava rock* and *metal plates* are an alternative to ceramic briquettes.

- **Charcoal briquettes:** The most common fuel for a live fire, manufactured from ground charcoal, coal dust, and starch. They are compressed into a uniform, pillow shape and packaged for sale in 5- to 50-pound bags.

- **Charcoal chimney starter:** A metal, cylinder-shaped container that is filled with newspaper and charcoal and used to quickly ignite a charcoal fire.

- **Charcoal grill:** A grill that uses charcoal as its principal fuel. A charcoal grill can be round, square, covered, uncovered, portable, or stationary. The most common type is a covered kettle grill.

- **Coal grate:** The rack that holds the charcoal in the firebox.

✔ **Cover:** Sometimes called the *hood,* a grill's cover is a lid that goes over your food and grill grid to keep moisture in the food. Most gas and charcoal grills come with a hinged or fully-removable cover.

✔ **Drip pan:** A metal pan placed under the food to catch drippings when grilling indirectly.

✔ **Electric grill:** An indoor or outdoor grill whose heat comes from electric coils.

✔ **Fire starters:** Any number of gadgets or materials, such as the chimney starter, electric coil, wax or gel cubes, or compressed wood, used to ignite charcoal.

✔ **Firebox:** The underbelly or bottom of the grill that holds the fire or heat.

✔ **Flare-ups:** Flames caused by fat dripping onto hot coals or lava rock.

✔ **Gas grill:** A grill whose heating source is gas from a propane tank (or occasionally, a main gas line).

✔ **Grid:** The latticework of metal rods where you place your food on a grill is called a *grid,* or a *grill grid.* (Weber confuses things a little by calling this area the *grate,* which everyone else calls the metal piece on which the charcoal sits.) One grid is included with every grill.

✔ **Grill baskets:** Hinged, wire baskets that ease the grilling (and turning) of sliced vegetables, a delicate piece of fish, burgers, and other foods.

✔ **Hibachi:** A small, portable, uncovered grill, often made of cast-iron. Great for beach or tailgate grilling.

✔ **Kettle grill:** A relatively inexpensive, round charcoal grill with a heavy cover. It stands on three legs and is excellent for either direct or indirect grilling.

✔ **Lava rock:** This long-lasting natural rock results from volcanic lava and is used as an alternative to ceramic briquettes. The irregularly shaped lava rock heats evenly in gas grills. Unlike charcoal briquettes, it can be used over and over.

✔ **Marinate:** To soak food in a seasoned liquid mixture in order to impart flavor to the food before it is cooked. The steeping liquid, often made with herbs, spices, oil, and an acidic ingredient like lemon juice or vinegar, is called a *marinade*.

- **Natural lump charcoal:** The carbon residue of wood that's been charred in a kiln — usually found in the form of chunks. This is one heating source for charcoal grills.

- **Roasting:** The process of cooking food in a pan in a closed-grill setup. By using indirect heat, you can roast an entire prime rib or turkey to perfection on a grill.

- **Rotisserie rod:** The spit or long metal skewer that suspends and rotates food over the grill's heat source.

- **Rub:** A concentrated, flavorful blend of dry or wet herbs, seasonings, and spices that's rubbed onto the surface of the food before grilling.

- **Sear:** To cook food directly above relatively high heat in order to seal in juices and give flavor, a brown color, and a slightly crusty surface.

- **Smoker box:** Small, perforated steel or cast-iron container, placed directly on the lava rocks or ceramic bricks of a gas grill, that holds flavored wood chips and provides smoke.

- **Vent:** The holes in a grill cover or firebox that open and close like a shutter. An open vent increases the oxygen and heat of a fire, while a closed vent does the opposite. Some grills don't have vents.

- **Wood chips and wood chunks:** Natural hardwood materials added to the fire to impart smoky flavor to food as it grills.

Chapter 2

Maintaining and Accessorizing Your Grill

. . . .

In This Chapter

▶ Cleaning and storing your grill

▶ Deciding which accessories you really need

. . . .

Regardless of what you cook on your grill, you want to make sure to properly care for your grill every time you use it. You need to do the same for all of your grilling accessories.

Long Live Your Grill

Although the outer units of most grills carry a lifetime guarantee, keeping your grill oiled and clean and storing it correctly are essential to a long, happy grill life.

Oiling the grids

Keeping your grill grid lightly oiled helps improve your grilling in two ways:

✔ Oiling prevents food ingredients from sticking while you're cooking.

✔ Oiling makes grid cleanup easier after each meal.

Use a little vegetable oil, wiped on with a soft cloth, to oil your grid. Or you can use one of those aerosol vegetable oil sprays on a cold — but never a hot — grill.

A clean grill is a good grill

Grills can last a lifetime if you take good care of them, as follows:

- ✔ You can clean some indoor electric grills in the dishwasher. Surprised? Electric grills have come a long way since their introduction in the late '80s. Many grills now carry a feature known as an *embedded-element,* which means that you don't have to mess with cleaning and caring for the heating element because it's buried in the innards of the unit — you don't ever see it. This also means that the grills have only one or two pieces — and the whole kit and caboodle can go straight into the dishwasher after dinner.

- ✔ When cleaning gas and charcoal grills, try the following:

  - • After each use, use a wire brush to clean off the food particles remaining on the grid. Close the lid of the grill and, if you have a gas grill, turn up the heat for about 10 minutes to burn off any excess food remaining on the grid.

  - • Periodically clean the grids with a solution of warm, soapy water, using nylon or plastic woven pads to avoid damaging the grid. Use non-abrasive scouring powder on stubborn stains if you wish, but a small amount of grease left on the grids helps preserve the metal — it will burn off the next time you use the grill. Cast-iron grids should be seasoned after cleaning by applying a light coating of oil.

  - • You may clean the interior of the grill with the same soapy solution or with a can of aerosol grill cleaner. Scour with a scrub brush and then rinse with water and air dry. Never use anything but soapy water on the exterior of the grill because a cleaner may damage the paint or porcelain.

- Your grill won't work properly if the burners become clogged, so if you see an uneven flame, remove the burner and clean the ports with a wire. You can also force water through the removed burner until you are sure that it is coming through each hole. If the burners rust to the point of showing cracks or breaks, buy new ones.

Storing your grill

By using an indoor electric grill, you can grill all year 'round, regardless of the weather. Between uses, simply store your grill in a kitchen cabinet.

When weather permits, gas and charcoal grill users can also grill during most of the year. If you decide to pack your grill away for the coldest winter months, though, you certainly can. Be sure to thoroughly clean your grill before storing it and — for a gas grill — make sure that the gas lines are completely and tightly closed off and that the gas cylinder is removed.

If storing your gas or charcoal grill indoors, always remove the propane cylinder and store it outside in a cool, shaded spot. Never, under any circumstances, store a propane cylinder inside your home or garage. Doing so could be deadly.

Tools and Toys

Step into a hardware store or kitchen gadget shop and you'll see an amazing array of tongs, brushes, and spatulas in a variety of shapes and configurations. In this section, we introduce you to timesaving, flavor-enhancing, safety-heightening accessories that no griller — beginner or guru — should be without. In most cases, we show you an illustration of the most common types; keep in mind, however, that manufacturers and prices affect the exact sizes, shapes, and features.

Think of these accessories as investments and purchase the best ones that you can afford. Premium accessories are apt to have heavy-duty finishes and strong, comfortable handles.

✔ **Tongs.** Tongs are essential equipment — they're a better choice than a long fork because you can flip food over without piercing the food (which can let out the juices) and they allow you to maneuver most foods better than a spatula does.

Buy with length in mind. Never use short, overly flexible ice tongs at the grill. A good pair of grilling tongs (see Figure 2-1) should be between 15 and 18 inches long and must have a wooden or insulated grip (hot metal burns!).

✔ **Fork and carving knife.** A good knife is not nearly as important as a good *fork* when you're grilling. And a good fork is not nearly as important as a *long* fork — 16 inches or more — with a wooden handle and two tines.

When moving around large pieces of meat — such as roasts — with a grill fork, try not to pierce the meat too deeply. By the same token, be careful not to spear the meat too delicately so that it falls off and causes flare-ups.

Given the fact that much of what comes off your grill (slabs of meat, ribs, or sausage) will need to be cut, invest in a good, heavy-handled, well-balanced carving knife, curved butcher's knife, or chef's knife.

spring-loaded tongs

Figure 2-1: Grilling tongs should be long and have a good, wide opening.

✔ **Spatula.** We never get tired of repeating ourselves on the issue of length: Use a spatula that is 15 to 18 inches long from the tip of the handle to the end of the blade. (See Figure 2-2.)

Also, be sure not to use the following:

- A Teflon or nonstick spatula for the kitchen used to flip pancakes, because it may burn or melt.

- An outdoor metal spatula with a metal handle. The handle will transfer heat to your hand.

- A long spatula used to spread icing on a cake. Such a tool is completely useless at a barbecue because it's too thin and flexible to hold a heavyweight piece of meat, poultry, or fish.

✔ **Grilling mitt.** We cannot stress enough the importance of a good grilling mitt. A dishtowel or fireproof pot holder just doesn't give you the protection you need to grill safely. The mitts should be flexible and allow you to pick pots, pans, skewers, and other items off the grill with ease.

Figure 2-2: A good grill spatula should be sturdy, with a fairly wide blade.

A mitt also should be long enough to reach past your elbow — the longer the better, at least 15 inches — and have a flame-retardant coating. (See Figure 2-3.) Long-lasting, sturdy mitts start at about $7 and can run as high as $20. If you can afford it, pay a bit extra to get a fully insulated, thick pair with a thumb.

✔ **Basting brushes and mops.** The most common *basting brush* (shown in Figure 2-4), is brush-shaped, sometimes with an angled brush head, and is very useful for all kinds of basting but is most often used for light basting sauces. The most important virtue of such a brush is its length; look for ones at least 16 inches long so that you can baste while the food is on the grill.

The bristles on a brush should be fairly pliable and extend at least 3 inches from the end of the handle. You don't need to spend much on a good brush, but don't spend too little either, or it will fall apart before long. Between $5 and $8 is a good range to look for.

A *basting mop,* sometimes called a *Texas-style barbecue brush,* also shown in Figure 2-4, is just that — a little cotton mop for quickly slathering on thick sauce. When soaked with barbecue sauce, this brush is not likely to catch on fire, but be attentive anyway.

✔ **Skewers.** Skewers, shown in Figure 2-5, are wonderful grill accessories, allowing you to cook and easily turn kebabs. (Check out Chapter 5 for some outstanding kebab recipes.) Skewers should be between 15 and 18 inches long. Skewers that are 6 to 8 inches long, however, are perfect for cocktail party kebabs.

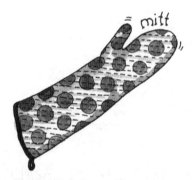

Figure 2-3: Use a thick, well-insulated, long, flexible mitt.

Figure 2-4: Mops and brushes for your food — not your kitchen floor.

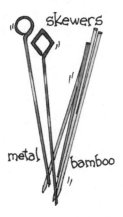

Figure 2-5: Skewers should be long and easy to pick up
so that you can turn them on the grill.

Bamboo skewers are popular and do a good job when you're grilling kebabs. Before using them, soak them in water for a half hour so that the ends don't catch fire.

✔ **Thermometer.** One of the single biggest challenges faced by inexperienced — and even many experienced — grillers is turning out food that is moist, juicy, and cooked to perfection, both inside and out. A good food *thermometer* tells you the temperature inside the food being cooked and will solve this problem for you. You can find two basic types of thermometers for use on a grill (see Figure 2-6):

- **Stainless steel insert thermometer:** This heat-resistant thermometer that you use for a roast in an oven works effectively on a grill, too. To use this thermometer, insert the stainless steel spike into the meat at the beginning of the cooking process and it registers the temperature on a glass-faced dial. This thermometer is intended only for foods that allow you to place the probe at least 2 to 2½ inches into the grilled food. It is not intended for use on steaks, chops, chicken breasts, or other thin food.

- **Instant-read thermometer:** This type of thermometer does exactly what it says; that is, you can insert it into the meat at any moment and get — you guessed it — an instant reading! You must immediately remove the thermometer, however. Some models even display digital numbers; you don't have to buy this type, but if you do, be sure that the numbers are easy to read.

Figure 2-6: Two types of thermometers work well at the grill — the instant-read and the stainless steel insert.

✔ **Grill topper.** A grill topper — sometimes called a *perforated grid, fish grid,* or *delicate foods grid* — is a porcelain grid with holes about half the size of a dime. (See Figure 2-7.) Place it on the grill grid (the one that comes with your grill, where you normally place the food) when you want to cook small foods (such as shrimp, scallops, delicate fish, mushrooms, and cut-up vegetables) that would otherwise fall into the fire. A grill topper makes it simple to turn delicate food. Lightly coating the food with oil makes the food even easier to turn.

Several varieties of electric grills have a griddle grid surface, which means that you can grill small foods without using a grill topper.

Grill toppers come in several different sizes, so consider the size of your grill grid before selecting one, because you may want room to cook other foods on the regular grid at the same time. Prices range from $15 to $30.

grill topper

Figure 2-7: A grill topper helps you grill delicate food.

Chapter 3

A Griller's Pantry

· ·

In This Chapter

▶ Concocting classic condiments

▶ Sorting out oils, vinegars, and wines

▶ Marinating for taste and tenderness

▶ Serving up savory sauces

▶ Massaging with tasty rubs

▶ Creating compound butters

· ·

*E*very grilling chef needs an arsenal of recipes for marinades, condiments, sauces, rubs, and compound butters — concoctions that elevate humble steaks, grilled chicken, pork chops, and hamburger into something more sublime. In this chapter, we share our recommended list of nonperishable items for your grilling pantry and give you recipes for several to make at home. All of them complement the unique flavors of grilled foods while adding taste, color, and pizzazz.

Kitchen Helpers — Bottled and Canned Goods

In a perfect world, every barbecue sauce and marinade would be made from scratch with the freshest of ingredients. But in this time-pressed world, we rely heavily on good commercial products. Having even a few of the following items on hand in your pantry or refrigerator allows you to whip up an assortment of barbecue sauces, dressings, and marinades in a hurry.

- **Bottled barbecue sauce:** Every year you can find new sauces flavored with hickory, mesquite, Jamaican jerk seasonings, habañero peppers, peaches and pineapple, bourbon, rum, and every kind of imaginable hot chile pepper. Barbecue sauces are not meant for ribs or chicken only. Use them to baste salmon, shrimp kebabs, pork, or lamb chops.

   Before purchasing a product for the first time, read the ingredient label to get a general idea of its flavor. Try to avoid products in which the primary ingredient is sugar, salt, or fat — or that's all you'll taste.

   Remember, most barbecue sauces are loaded with sugar and should be applied only during the last 10 to 15 minutes of cooking to prevent the food from charring.

- **Bottled marinades, dressings, and other basting and finishing sauces:** These ingredients provide the grilling cook tremendous variety and convenience. Bottled vinaigrette can substitute as a last-minute marinade for poultry, vegetables, or pork. Check out the many Asian and Thai-style products including sauces for kebabs, poultry, and ribs.

- **Mayonnaise:** No kitchen pantry is complete without a jar of mayonnaise, but for the most part, think of mayonnaise as an incomplete dressing. We like to add a range of ingredients to mayonnaise, such as sun-dried tomatoes, basil, mustard, horseradish, rosemary, Tabasco sauce, or grated lemon peel, to create a whole assortment of dressings, sauces, and spreads.

- **Soy sauce:** A vital ingredient in so many flavorful marinades, basting sauces, barbecue sauces, and dressings. Soy sauce adds distinctive flavor, brown color, and saltiness. Light soy sauce is sodium-reduced and therefore less salty. You can substitute this anytime for soy sauce when less salt is preferred.

- **Worcestershire sauce:** This sauce is a combination of vinegar, molasses, water, sugar, anchovies, and other savory ingredients. Add Worcestershire sauce according to your taste to marinades, dressings, basting sauces, or hamburger patties; splash over finished grilled foods such as steaks, lamb chops, poultry, or roasted potatoes.

Sweetening sauces and marinades

When preparing a sauce or a condiment, you may want it to be boldly sweet, or you may want just a hint of sweet taste. Much like salt, sweet ingredients, used in moderation, can help blend all the other flavors within a recipe.

✔ **Honey:** Honey can add anywhere from a slight to an overwhelming element of sweetness to marinades and basting sauces, and it mixes particularly well with Asian ingredients like soy sauce, ginger, hoisin sauce, garlic, and sesame oil.

Like other sweeteners, however, honey can cause grilled food to char and burn. For the best effect, apply any basting sauces containing honey only during the final minutes of grilling.

✔ **Molasses:** A common ingredient in barbecue sauces, molasses adds sweetness and color to marinades and barbecue and basting sauces.

✔ **Light and dark brown sugar:** Brown sugar is white sugar combined with molasses to give it color and moisture. The lighter the color, the less intense (or less molasses-like) the flavor.

✔ **Fruit jams and preserves:** Jams and preserves enhance grilled foods as ingredients in glazes and finishing sauces.

Condiment-ry, My Dear Watson

A *condiment* is any small side dish or accompaniment to food that adds flavor, texture, and contrasting color. Condiments can be vinegary (like ketchup), sweet (like preserved watermelon rind), hot and spicy (like salsa), sour (like dill pickles), or salty (like sun-dried tomatoes). The following list is a few of our favorites, available in any major supermarket.

✔ **Chutneys:** These sweet, tart, and spicy combinations of cooked fruits or vegetables make delectable accompaniments to grilled foods. Keep bottles of store-bought mango or tomato chutney on hand as a last-minute topping for grilled burgers, steaks, poultry, lamb, or pork. Or, make your own.

Tomato Chutney

This recipe treats tomatoes like the fruits they are — sweetening them with brown sugar — to make a chutney that's great with grilled foods. If you want, remove the tomato skins before making the chutney. To do this, plunge the whole tomatoes into boiling water for about 15 seconds or until the skins begin to split. Then chill in a bowl of ice water before slipping off the skins.

Preparation time: *15 minutes*

Yield: *About 2 cups*

2 tablespoons olive oil

1 onion, peeled and chopped

½ cup light brown sugar, packed

3 tablespoons apple cider vinegar

½ to 1 large jalapeño pepper, seeded and chopped

3 cups peeled, seeded, and chopped tomatoes

½ teaspoon fresh ginger, peeled and grated

1 In a medium sauté pan or skillet, heat the oil over medium heat; add the onion and cook for 7 minutes or until lightly browned and very soft, stirring occasionally.

2 Add the brown sugar, vinegar, and jalapeño pepper; cook for 4 to 5 minutes, stirring occasionally until the mixture is dark brown and syrupy.

3 Stir in the tomatoes, raise the heat to medium-high, and boil gently for 5 more minutes or until the liquid is reduced and the mixture has thickened. Remove from heat and stir in the ginger, adding more to taste (if desired). Serve warm, or cover and chill.

Go-With! *This chutney goes well with grilled beef, poultry, or pork.*

- ✔ **Horseradish:** A delicious condiment for grilled fish, horseradish also adds zing to dressings, dips, and sauces made with ketchup, sour cream, or mayonnaise.

- ✔ **Ketchup:** Ketchup is the ultimate ying-yang of condiments — a blend of tangy vinegar, sweeteners like sugar or corn syrup, and pureed tomatoes. Before being knocked off its throne by the now more popular salsa, ketchup was America's favorite condiment. Dress it up by adding chopped scallions, minced ginger, or horse-radish. Or use ketchup as an ingredient in marinades, basting sauces, and salsas.

✔ **Mustards:** There are really two types of prepared mustards: those that are creamy smooth and those that contain coarse seeds. Either type may be flavored with herbs and spices, red or white wine, champagne, honey, sugar, chiles, or peppercorns.

✔ **Salsa:** Although salsas are usually tomato-based, the salsa product line is growing to include salsas with roasted corn, red pepper, black olives, and other ingredients. Store varieties range from mild to hot. Use salsa as a quick condiment for hot dogs, grilled burgers, steaks, chicken, or fish. Try it as a spread for quesadillas, fajitas, or other sandwich wraps. Add it to vegetable salads made with chopped tomatoes, corn, or canned beans. Use it to add flavor and heat to creamy macaroni salads.

Fresh Tomato Salsa

Fortunately for us, juicy, ripe tomatoes come to market just when the grilling season really kicks into gear.

Preparation time: *15 minutes*

Yield: *About 2 cups*

2 large ripe tomatoes, seeded and diced	*½ to 1 jalapeño pepper, seeded and chopped*
1 small onion, peeled and diced	*1 ½ tablespoons olive oil*
1 clove garlic, peeled and minced	*Juice of half a lime*
3 tablespoons chopped fresh cilantro or parsley	*Salt and pepper to taste*
	Tabasco sauce to taste

In a small mixing bowl, combine all the ingredients. Cover and let stand at room temperature for at least 15 minutes before serving.

Vary It! *Substitute 2 tablespoons tequila for the lime juice.*

- ✔ **Sun-dried tomatoes:** Sold either as oil-packed or dried, sun-dried tomatoes are somewhat chewy and intensely flavored. You can use them to flavor salads, dressings, and spreads.

- ✔ **Tabasco sauce:** An all-purpose spicy seasoning and condiment made from hot capsicum peppers, vinegar, and salt, Tabasco sauce adds heat and a pleasant sharpness to marinades, dressings, and finished grilled foods.

Oils, Vinegars, and Wines — Demystified

Oils range in taste from the nearly neutral flavor of ever-so-subtle peanut oil, to bold and buttery olive oil, to nutty, almost bitter-tasting, dark sesame oil. Avoid exposing oils to light and air, because they cause the oils to deteriorate more rapidly — always store oils in a cool, dark place. Keep oil containers tightly sealed after opening and use within several months to one year. Throw out any oils that develop a musty or rancid smell.

- ✔ **Olive oil:** Use olive oil in dressings, marinades, and basting and finishing sauces. Olive oil is indispensable to the grilling chef — it infuses marinades, dressings, sauces, and salsas with its rich, fruity flavor. Try olive oil drizzled over grilled breads, grilled vegetables, roasted red peppers, and all kinds of grilled chicken or fish.

- ✔ **Sesame oil:** Made from sesame seeds, sesame oil has a rich, distinctive flavor. Use it sparingly to accent marinades made with Asian ingredients like soy sauce, ginger, and garlic.

- ✔ **Nut oils:** Extracted from roasted walnuts, almonds, hazelnuts, and other nuts, these oils are very expensive and rich in flavor. Delicious in salad dressings and some salsas, especially when the recipe uses the nut as an ingredient. However, they are highly perishable and must be refrigerated.

Peanut, corn, safflower, soy, and other mild vegetable oils can be mixed with equal amounts of olive oil to enrich their flavors.

Flavored oils — the slick solution

Flavored oils, seasoned with an assortment of ingredients such as lemon slices, whole peppercorns, dried herbs, garlic, and chiles, are terrific drizzled over grilled breads, grilled pizzas, grilled vegetables, or grilled steaks, fish, chicken, lamb, or vegetables.

Use either of the following oils to generously brush 1½ to 2 pounds of steak, chicken, fish, or pork. Brush both sides before grilling. Refrigerate for 1 to 2 hours (or even less, if you don't have the time).

✔ **Lemon-Rosemary Oil:** Because you must make this oil with fresh rosemary, you may decide to plant a rosemary pot in a sunny outdoor spot, or even indoors on a kitchen windowsill. Infuse the oil with rosemary and other seasonings by pureeing all ingredients in a blender. Whirl until smooth 6 tablespoons olive oil, ¼ cup minced rosemary leaves, 3 cloves peeled and crushed garlic, 2 teaspoons lemon juice, and 2 teaspoons grated lemon peel. Brush this oil on about 2 pounds of sirloin steaks or tender beef kebabs; on fish fillets or fish steaks; on boneless chicken breasts; or on sea scallop kebabs.

✔ **Mustard-Worcestershire Oil:** Spoon ¼ cup Dijon-style mustard in a small mixing bowl. Add ½ cup olive oil in a slow, steady stream, beating constantly with a fork or wire whisk to blend the mustard into the oil until the sauce is smooth and creamy. Whisk in 2 teaspoons Worcestershire sauce (or more or less to taste). Season to taste with salt and pepper. Brush this sharp, mustard-flavored oil on pieces of chicken, fish, pork, or tender cuts of lamb or beef before grilling.

Be sure to discard all unused oil. In a short time, the fresh ingredients you add to the oil become a breeding ground for harmful bacteria, so toss it out as soon as you've finished coating the food.

Vinegars tenderize cuts of meat as they marinate, but they also add a pleasant tartness to sauces, dressings, and marinades. Vinegars are almost always paired with oils to balance their harshness. We are partial to balsamic vinegar, which is slightly sweet, less harsh, and more complex in flavor than other vinegars. If by accident you add too much vinegar to a dressing or marinade, you can tone down the acidic effect by adding a pinch of salt, more oil, or by whisking in a bit of sugar or other sweetener, such as honey, to taste. Here are some types of vinegar to keep in your pantry:

✔ **Balsamic vinegar:** Bold, rich, and slightly sweet, real balsamic vinegar is outrageously expensive and made only in the area near Modena, Italy. Most of the bottles sold in the supermarkets are imitations. But being a "fake" doesn't mean it's bad, it's just less aged. Balsamic vinegar is delicious in marinades, dressings, and finishing sauces. Try splashing it to taste on grilled lamb, chicken, or pork.

✔ **Apple cider vinegar:** Good for almost all recipes where vinegar is an ingredient, apple cider vinegar is especially good with marinades and dressings that contain a fruit or citrus juice or that have an element of sweetness.

✔ **White wine vinegar:** This type of vinegar can be fruity or very dry. It's delicious in relishes and chutneys to counterbalance sweet flavorings.

✔ **Red wine vinegar:** Use this bold and pleasantly pungent vinegar in marinades for beef, pork, or poultry.

✔ **Rice vinegar:** Slightly milder than other vinegars, rice vinegar works well with sherry or sake in marinades.

Like vinegars, all wines are tenderizing agents, but their chief function in a marinade or sauce is to add bold flavor. For marinades or sauces, you don't need to spend more than about $8 on a good bottle of red or white wine — and at that price, whatever wine remains in the bottle is good enough for serving with the meal.

✔ **Dry red and white wine:** These acid-based ingredients are tenderizing agents, but more importantly, they add a complexity of flavor to marinades and basting sauces. Add herbs and spices according to taste and always have an oil component in a red or white wine marinade to take off some of the acidic edge.

✔ **Marsala:** A *fortified* wine (which means that another alcohol, such as brandy, has been added to the wine to raise its alcohol content), Marsala is good in marinades for poultry and game birds, adding a tinge of sweetness.

✔ **Sake:** A Japanese alcoholic beverage made from fermented rice, sake is excellent in marinades. You can use it as a substitute for dry vermouth or pale dry sherry. After it's opened, it can be stored in the refrigerator for 3 to 4 weeks.

✔ **Sherry:** Sherry is a fortified wine, which essentially means that it is an aged blend of different wines and brandy. Depending on its sweetness, sherry is labeled dry, medium dry, or sweet. Sherry can be used in marinades and basting sauces to flavor poultry, pork, or beef.

The Magic of Marinades

The typical marinade is a combination of an oil, an acid, herbs, and spices. The fat that lubricates and moisturizes the food is usually a vegetable oil. The acid component may be a vinegar, lemon juice, or other citric acid, yogurt, or wine. Although these acids don't actually tenderize the food, they can soften the surface tissues of tougher cuts.

Marinades come in endless flavors — spicy, sweet, savory, tangy, herby, oily, acidic, salty, and so forth. We give you several marinades in this chapter and throughout the book, but there's no reason to use only our recipes. What you put into the marinade is a matter of personal taste — if you feel like experimenting on your own, use the marinade combinations that follow as guidelines, adjusting specific ingredient amounts to mix a potion that works for you.

When breaking away from a recipe to blend your own marinade, always consider the food that's being soaked:

✔ **Is it lean — for example, chicken breast or white fish?**

As a rule, the leaner the food, the better it does in marinades with a fairly high concentration of oil.

✔ **Is it high in fat, like the well-marbled red meat of a ribeye steak?**

Richer foods hold their own against more robust acidic ingredients like red wine vinegar or wine.

And think about how ingredients work best together:

✔ Soy sauce is compatible with the flavors of ginger, sesame oil, scallions, and garlic. Spicy Asian-flavored marinades for fish, pork, beef, or chicken often combine dark soy sauce, rice vinegar, garlic, sugar, chiles, fresh ginger, peanut oil, scallions, and coriander leaves.

✔ White or red wines mix well with olive oil, chopped garlic, onions, or shallots, and fresh herbs such as tarragon, thyme, and rosemary or bay leaf. Red wine marinades are good with beef, game, and dark-meat poultry.

✔ Fresh or dried chiles, chili powder, cayenne pepper, crushed red pepper, and Tabasco sauce can punch up the flavor in a marinade and leave your mouth with an appealing hot and spicy aftertaste.

✔ Honey, molasses, brown sugar, and granulated sugar add sweetness to your grilled foods. Compose a tasty marinade for all kinds of poultry by mixing together corn oil, ketchup or molasses, dry sherry, Worcestershire sauce, soy sauce, crushed garlic, chopped onions, Tabasco sauce, salt, and pepper (all to your tastes).

✔ Peanut oil is very mild, while sesame oil is bold and best if used in limited amounts in a marinade.

✔ Grated lemon, lime, or orange peel is rich in aromatic citrus oil and can be used quite liberally in marinades.

✔ Garlic — whole, minced, or pressed — seems to improve nearly every savory marinade.

✔ Dijon-style mustard added to a marinade of dry white wine, olive oil, fresh lemon juice, lemon peel, and chopped fresh herbs like parsley, rosemary, basil, or thyme is delicious for poultry or fish.

✔ Yogurt is a mild acid that blends nicely with cumin, turmeric, curry, cayenne pepper, ginger, paprika, chopped onion, and garlic to coat and flavor kebabs of lamb, chicken, or fish.

✔ Contrary to what's written in many other cookbooks, adding salt to a marinade does not compel food to release its natural juices, nor does it cause food to toughen or dry out. Water or liquid flows towards those cells that are the most dense or concentrated, in a natural effort to dilute them. The cell walls of the food sitting in the marinade take in mostly liquid and very little salt. So, if you wish, add the salt.

As a general rule, you need about 1 to 2 cups of marinade for every 1½ to 2 pounds of food. You want enough marinade to completely surround the food. Most foods, except for delicate fish, vegetables, and certain cuts of tender meat, benefit from several hours of marinating time, and many foods like to stand in the liquid overnight. Turn over the food in the marinade (or the plastic bag) a few times to moisten all the food surfaces.

Select a container that's the proper size and shape — in which the food fits snugly and is immersed in the liquid. You can use a mixing bowl for your marinade, but make sure that it's glass, ceramic, or plastic, because acidic ingredients and alcohol can react with aluminum and iron, giving the meat and liquid a metallic flavor and gray color. However, we think a large, resealable plastic bag works best. Just mix the marinade right in the bag, toss in the food, seal the bag, and chill, turning occasionally. Foods marinated in a bag take up less room in your refrigerator.

Very often the same marinade that's used to soak the uncooked food can be reheated and poured over the grilled food to serve as a delicious finishing sauce. However, if any kind of raw fish, meat, or poultry was first soaked in the marinade, then it must be heated to boiling and allowed to simmer a minute or two to destroy any possible bacteria from the raw food.

Spicy Soy and Cilantro Marinade

This marinade is delicious with any cut of beef and also works with chicken, fish, or pork. Any leftover marinade can be boiled for a finishing sauce or tossed into cooked noodles with just enough additional peanut oil and soy sauce to coat.

Preparation time: *15 minutes*

Yield: *About 1⅓ cups*

½ cup dark soy sauce

¼ cup plus 2 tablespoons rice vinegar

¼ cup peanut oil

¼ cup chopped cilantro leaves

4 cloves garlic, peeled and chopped

3 scallions, trimmed and chopped (white and green parts)

1 tablespoon plus 1 teaspoon peeled, grated fresh ginger

2 teaspoons sugar

1 to 2 chile peppers, seeded and finely minced

Combine all the ingredients in a small mixing bowl or measuring cup and pour over 1½ to 2 pounds of meat, chicken, or fish. For best results, marinate fish for 30 minutes to 1 hour, and other foods for 6 hours or overnight, turning occasionally.

Gingery Grilled Vegetable Marinade

This vegetable marinade combines soy sauce, ginger, and sesame oil with the zing of Tabasco sauce and is especially delicious with tomatoes, onions, summer squash (zucchini or yellow squash), and mushrooms. (See Chapter 8 for more information on grilling vegetables.)

Preparation time: *25 minutes*

Marinating time: *30 minutes to 1 hour*

Yield: *6 servings*

½ cup white wine vinegar

⅓ cup light soy sauce

6 tablespoons olive oil

2 tablespoons sesame oil

2 tablespoons peeled and minced fresh ginger

1 tablespoon brown sugar, packed

2 large cloves garlic, peeled and minced

2 teaspoons Tabasco sauce

Salt and pepper to taste

6 to 7 cups sliced vegetables

1 In a medium mixing bowl or glass measuring cup, make the marinade by combining all the ingredients except the vegetables.

2 Place the sliced vegetables in a 1-gallon, resealable plastic bag or other large container; pour the marinade over the vegetables in the bag or container.

3 Press the air out of the bag and seal tightly, or cover the container. Refrigerate for 30 minutes to 1 hour, turning the bag over once or occasionally tossing the vegetables in the container.

4 Place vegetables on an oiled grill grid. Grilling time will depend on the thickness of the vegetables.

Ignore the advice of cookbooks and recipes that instruct you to marinate meat, fish, or poultry at room temperature for 2 to 3 hours before grilling. You can safely marinate meat, fish, or poultry at room temperature for only about 30 minutes; after that, you risk the danger of contamination from airborne bacteria. Be on the safe side: Keep foods well chilled in the refrigerator. Grilling chilled meats takes a little longer, but you avoid the possibility of contaminating your food.

The Secret's in the Sauce

When you grill, the wonderful cooking juices that ordinarily end up in the pan (with top of stove or oven roasting techniques) are lost into the fire. To compensate for this sad fact, grilling gurus — like yourself — keep a file of quick and easy sauces that add a last-minute finish to that sizzling steak, chop, piece of chicken, or fish fillet. In this section, we give you a few of our favorite sauce recipes for all kinds of grilled foods.

Creamy Horseradish Sauce

This sauce combines sour cream, horseradish, fresh lemon juice, and ripe, chopped tomatoes.

Preparation time: *10 minutes*

Yield: *About ⅔ cup*

½ cup sour cream

¼ cup chopped ripe tomatoes

2 tablespoons bottled horseradish, drained

1 tablespoon mayonnaise

2 teaspoons fresh lemon juice

Pepper to taste

Combine all the ingredients in a small bowl; cover and chill until ready to serve.

Vary It! *You can substitute 3 tablespoons peeled and chopped cucumber or scallions for the tomato. Or for a snappy raw vegetable dip, add 2 tablespoons ketchup or chili sauce, and Tabasco sauce to taste.*

Go-With! *This sauce is terrific with grilled sausage, fish steaks, shellfish, burgers, or poultry.*

Pesto Sauce

Here is our favorite pesto recipe. For a lemony pesto that also works well with grilled shrimp and other fish, stir the grated peel of half a lemon into the finished sauce.

Preparation time: *15 minutes*

Yield: *About ½ cup*

2 cups, loosely packed fresh basil leaves, stems removed (about 2 ounces)

½ cup extra-virgin olive oil

3 tablespoons pine nuts or walnuts

3 large cloves garlic, peeled and chopped

Salt and pepper to taste

¼ cup grated Parmesan cheese

1 Rinse and pat dry the trimmed basil leaves.

2 In the container of a food processor or blender combine basil leaves, oil, pine nuts or walnuts, garlic, and salt and pepper. Blend to a fine texture but not a smooth puree, stopping once to scrape down the sides of the container.

3 Add the Parmesan cheese and blend for just a few more seconds. Cover and chill until ready to use.

Rub-a-Dub-Dub

Rubs are usually a dry combination of herbs and spices, although sometimes a little oil is added to moisten the mixture. You simply massage rubs onto the surface of the food and end up with a wonderful crispness to the crust. Rubs are fast becoming the darlings of the grilling cook because, unlike marinades, they can be applied just before the food is grilled. However, if you have the time, let the food absorb the spice mixture in the refrigerator for several hours or overnight. Small tender pieces of fish or shellfish will benefit from about 30 minutes of standing time. A whole, spice-rubbed turkey should be plastic-wrapped to hold the rub tightly against its skin and then refrigerated overnight.

Rubs that are completely dry, without any oil or liquid ingredient, can be stored indefinitely in airtight containers in a cool, dry place. The amount of rub used to cover the surface of a piece of meat is entirely a matter of taste, but we suggest about 1 tablespoon for every pound of food.

To help the rub cling to the food's surface, apply it to food that is either completely dry or coated with a little oil. When seasoning poultry, spread the rub evenly over the surface and also under the skin as much as possible, being careful not to tear it.

Hot and Sweet Spice Rub

This rub gives an interesting sweet and spicy flavor to all kinds of meat.

Preparation time: *5 minutes*

Yield: *2 tablespoons*

2 teaspoons chili powder	*¼ teaspoon ground cinnamon*
1 teaspoon paprika	*¼ teaspoon ground allspice*
1 teaspoon brown sugar, firmly packed	*Pinch of pepper*
½ teaspoon flour	*Kosher or table salt (optional)*
½ teaspoon garlic salt	

Combine all ingredients and use as a rub for 2 to 2½ pounds of beef, poultry, or pork. Coat the food lightly with oil before applying. Sprinkle grilled food lightly with additional kosher or table salt before serving (if desired).

Pepper and Herb Rub

Here's a tasty all-purpose rub that's good with pork, poultry, or beef.

Preparation time: *10 minutes*

Yield: *About 3 tablespoons, or enough for about 2 to 2½ pounds of pork, chicken, or beef*

1 tablespoon paprika	½ teaspoon dried thyme
1 teaspoon garlic powder	½ teaspoon dried oregano leaves
1 teaspoon cayenne pepper	½ to ¾ teaspoon salt
½ teaspoon onion powder (optional)	¼ teaspoon black pepper
½ teaspoon ground white pepper (optional)	2 teaspoons grated lemon peel

1 Brush the food generously with vegetable or olive oil on all sides before rubbing with the herb mixture.

2 In a jar with a tight-fitting lid, combine all ingredients except the lemon peel. Add the grated lemon peel just before rubbing on chops, ribs, tenderloins, or kebabs. If you have the time, cover the rubbed food with plastic wrap and refrigerate for 30 minutes to 2 hours before grilling.

Compounding Your Options

Compound butter is butter that's dressed up with a few herbs, spices, or other intense seasonings. A small pat on a sizzling steak can increase the pleasure of a beefy meal. Compound butters are great with all sorts of foods, including grilled meats, fish, poultry, and many vegetables, and are more appropriate than a heavy sauce in warm weather.

Compound Butter

Prepare according to Figure 3-1. Following this basic compound butter recipe is a list of tasty variations.

Steps for Making Compound Butters

Put the butter in a bowl and let it get soft... but DON'T MELT IT!

Use a fork to blend in your seasonings!

Turn butter out, onto a piece of waxed paper and roll into a uniform cylinder.

Refrigerate or freeze and cut off pats as you need them.

Figure 3-1: Compounding your butter options.

Preparation time: 15 minutes

Yield: 4 servings

1 stick of softened, unsalted butter   Herbs and spices to taste

1 Use a food processor, blender, or sharp chef's knife to grind up or finely mince the seasonings.

2 Using a rubber spatula, wooden spoon, or your hands and a small bowl, soften the butter until it's malleable but not too soft.

3 Work in the seasonings with a fork or with your hands.

4 Spoon the mixture onto a sheet of waxed paper and use the paper to shape the butter mixture into a cylinder or log that has a diameter of about 2 inches.

5 Wrap well and refrigerate or freeze until ready to use. The butter keeps frozen for 1 to 2 months. When ready to use, simply slice off into butter pats 1- to 1½-inches thick.

6 Place a pat of butter on top of a thick steak, boneless grilled chicken breasts, or grilled fish; or toss grilled vegetables with butter to taste.

Vary It! In place of "herbs and spices to taste" in the Compound Butter recipe, substitute the following:

- **Lemon and Fresh Herb Butter:** Use 2 tablespoons finely chopped herbs (such as dill, basil, tarragon, thyme, marjoram, parsley, or sage), 1 teaspoon fresh lemon juice, 1 clove garlic, peeled and minced, and salt and pepper to taste. This butter works well with fish, pork, chicken, beef, and roasted vegetables.

- **Spicy Chili Butter:** Sprinkle in 1½ teaspoons chili powder, ¼ teaspoon paprika, 8 drops Tabasco sauce, and salt and pepper to taste. This butter is delicious with grilled corn, chicken, or fish or as a spread for grilled breads.

- **Ginger and Scallion Butter:** Use 3 tablespoons finely chopped scallions, 2 teaspoons peeled and grated fresh ginger (or ¾ teaspoon ground ginger), a pinch of garlic salt, and salt and pepper to taste. Try this butter with fish, pork, and grilled vegetables.

Chapter 4

Burgers and Sausages and Hot Dogs — Oh My!

*B*elieve it or not, you can serve a great burger, hot dog, or sausage with as much finesse as you may serve duck or lobster. For, even though these may seem like the easiest, slap-'em-on-the-grill kind of dishes, they can be made well or poorly. In this chapter, however, we give you the basics of turning out the kind of burgers, hot dogs, and sausages that make your guests think that you've gone to great lengths or know some long-hidden secrets!

Everyone Loves a Burger

A hamburger that has been carefully shaped and plumped to a proper thickness, grilled to a perfect medium-rare, with a slightly charred exterior, set on top of a toasted bun, and served with homemade condiments is a grand, glorious, and very simple food.

When people are disappointed with the results of grilled hamburgers, it's usually for two reasons: Either the burger patty is too thick to begin with and cooks to a frazzle on the edges, while remaining too pink or even raw in the middle, or the patty meat is too lean.

That tops the burger

In addition to down-home, old-fashioned ketchup, here are some of our favorite toppings:

- **A slice of cheese.** Try Cheddar, Swiss, Muenster, Gruyère, or fontina — any cheese that melts into a thin, velvety layer.

- **Tomato slices.** See Chapter 8 for tips on grilling tomatoes.

- **Raw or grilled onion slices.** Yellow onions are great, but so are milder red onions.

- **A dollop of fruit chutney.** Try adding a generous dollop of tomato, peach, or mango chutney. (Flip to Chapter 3 for more information on chutney.) It's a nice counterpoint to grilled meat.

- **Avocado.** Slice or mash ripe avocado into a spread with a little lemon juice and Tabasco sauce.

- **Pesto sauce.** Buy it or make your own. (Refer to Chapter 3 for a recipe.) For a smoky flavor, spread pesto sauce on the buns before toasting them on the grill.

- **Crisp strips of bacon.** You can add bacon with or without the lettuce and tomato.

- **Sautéed or grilled mushrooms.** Portobello mushrooms, with their meatlike texture and woodsy taste, are terrific sliced, brushed with oil, and grilled.

- **Pickles.** Choose from dill or sweet pickle slices.

- **Salsa.** Try making your own (see Chapter 3) or use any of the better bottled brands, such as Newman's Own Salsa.

Although your choice of burger meat is a matter of personal preference, we believe that the juiciest hamburgers are made with ground beef that is about 80 to 85 percent meat and 15 to 20 percent fat. This is about the ratio that you find in chuck — the best all-around cut for a perfect, juicy hamburger.

Try to mold the meat into a uniform, fairly flat patty, no thicker than ¾ inch. A thicker patty, mounded high in the center, is less likely to cook evenly — though we have to admit that big, fat burgers don't taste half bad. And be sure not to press the patty with the flat side of a spatula as it grills, even though you may be tempted to do so. Pressing squeezes out the flavorful juices and can also cause dangerous flare-ups.

Basic Burger

Ah, there's nothing like a beautifully grilled burger. This isn't your run-of-the-mill, gotta-grab-a-quick-bite burger. This is the kind of burger that you'll think about long after it's gone.

Preparation time: *15 minutes*

Grilling time: *10 to 15 minutes*

Yield: *4 servings*

1½ pounds ground chuck	¼ teaspoon pepper
¼ teaspoon salt, or to taste	4 hamburger buns

1 Combine the ground chuck, salt, and pepper in a medium mixing bowl, mixing lightly but thoroughly, using your hands. Shape the mixture into four patties, each ¾-inch thick in the center and at the edges. (Even thickness ensures even cooking and prevents the edges from drying out before the center is cooked.)

2 Place the patties on an oiled grill grid. Grill for 5 to 7 minutes per side for medium, less for rare to medium-rare, and 7 to 9 minutes per side for well done, turning once. (According to the U.S. Department of Agriculture, all ground meat should be cooked to at least medium doneness — 160° — or until the center of the patty is no longer pink.) Make a small incision in the center of each patty to determine doneness.

3 Toast the buns by placing them, split side down, on the edges of the grill grid for about 1 minute or until lightly browned.

4 Remove the burgers from the grill and serve on toasted hamburger buns.

Go-With! *The perfect grilled side dish for hamburgers is — hands down — corn on the cob. Check out Chapter 8 for all sorts of interesting ways to grill vegetables.*

Brush the grill grid with vegetable oil or nonstick cooking spray to prevent food from sticking to the grid. To avoid dangerous flare-ups, brush the grid *before* preheating the grill.

Keep in mind that all grilling temperatures are only estimates. Variables — such as the intensity of your grill's heat and the thickness of the meat — all affect the exact time it takes to cook your burger. To avoid overcooking, test the interior color of your burger. Do this by making a small incision with a thin knife in the center of the patty 1 or 2 minutes before you're done grilling.

Several grilling cookbooks recommend bringing ground meat to room temperature before placing it on the grill. We disagree. Instead, keep ground meat in the refrigerator until just before grilling. This minimizes exposure to airborne bacteria. And always place cooked burgers on a clean plate. Never return them to the plate used to carry them to the grill because it may be contaminated with bacteria from the uncooked meat.

Vary It! Use the following hamburger variations to spark your own burger creations. Each of these seasoning combinations works for 1½ pounds of raw ground meat.

- **Italian Burger:** Add the following ingredients to the ground meat mixture: 1 egg yolk, ¼ cup grated onion, 1 large clove garlic minced, 2 tablespoons chopped fresh basil or 2 teaspoons dried crushed basil, ½ teaspoon dried oregano, and salt and pepper to taste. Place grated Parmesan cheese on top of each burger (if desired) about 2 minutes before the burger is done and grill until the cheese melts.

- **Mexican Burger:** Add the following ingredients to the ground meat mixture: ¼ cup finely chopped onion, ½ to 1 teaspoon seeded and chopped jalapeño pepper, ¾ teaspoon ground cumin, and salt and pepper to taste. Serve on toasted buns or in warmed tortillas with a prepared tomato salsa or taco sauce, and slices of ripe avocado.

- **Asian Spiced Burger:** Add the following ingredients to the ground meat mixture: ¼ cup finely chopped scallions; 3 tablespoons teriyaki sauce; 1 large clove garlic, minced; and salt and pepper to taste.

Simple Sausage and Fancy Franks

Sausage-making is a food art practiced around the world. Sold fresh (or uncooked), cooked, smoked, and cured, sausages are made with a variety of meats and seasonings and shaped into links that vary in thickness and length.

Although many sausages are cured and/or cooked, they cannot be held indefinitely in warm weather. It is always best to preserve their flavor and quality by placing them in the coldest part of your refrigerator — 36° to 40° is the ideal temperature range. Freezing sausages is not a good idea, because the sausages lose flavor, but if you do freeze them, place them in vaporproof plastic bags and thaw them overnight in the refrigerator. The flavor really starts to decline after about two months of freezing, so don't leave them in the freezer any longer than that.

There's no trick to grilling franks and sausages; the cooking time is all you need to know.

- Uncooked sausage needs to be precooked before grilling to release some of the natural fat, which can cause dangerous flare-ups on the grill.

  To do this, prick each sausage several times and then simmer in water (flavored, if you wish, with wine, beer, or apple juice) for 5 to 10 minutes or until they're fully cooked with no trace of pink in the center. Grill until browned and crisp on all sides, turning often.

- Cooked sausages need only a few minutes of grilling to acquire that lovely, smoky taste and the bubbly skin that makes them irresistible on a summer afternoon.

- Remember to keep turning sausages — whether they are precooked or fresh — because they can burn very quickly.

- Grill frankfurters for about 8 minutes or until browned on all sides, turning frequently.

Grilled Kielbasa with Creamy Mustard Sauce

Make these kielbasa when you need dinner on the table in just a few minutes or when you're tailgating in the stadium parking lot of your favorite team.

Preparation time: *30 minutes*

Grilling time: *10 minutes*

Yield: *4 servings*

¼ cup sour cream	Pepper to taste
3 tablespoons Dijon-style mustard	Tabasco sauce (optional)
2 tablespoons prepared horseradish, drained	1 to 1¼ pounds fully cooked sausage (such as kielbasa or knackwurst)

1 Prepare the Creamy Mustard Sauce by combining the sour cream, mustard, horseradish, pepper, and Tabasco sauce (if desired) in a small bowl. Cover and refrigerate.

2 Slice the sausages, if necessary, into 4 pieces of equal length. Arrange the sausages on a lightly oiled grill grid. Grill, turning 2 or 3 times, until well browned on all sides and warmed through, about 10 minutes.

3 Divide the sausages among 4 individual plates and top each link with a generous dollop of Creamy Mustard Sauce.

Go-With! *Try serving the kielbasa sandwich-style, between wedges of crusty Italian bread.*

Chapter 5

Swordplay — Grilling Kebabs

Kebabs are some of the simplest and most popular foods to grill — you simply thread morsels of pork, beef, chicken, or other foods onto a skewer before grilling. In this chapter, we help you find the right skewer for your needs, give you hints for threading food onto those skewers, and share a few delicious recipes.

Ladies and Gentlemen — Choose Your Skewers!

Kebabs can't exist without skewers, so before you can grill kebabs, you need to choose your skewers. (Check out Chapter 2 for more information and illustrations on the different types of skewers available.) When buying skewers for your own use, you can choose between metal and wood, both of which have advantages and disadvantages:

✔ Metal skewers tend to be long — ranging from 10 to 18 inches long — so that you can pack them with food.

✔ Metal skewers are either flat, which makes sliding the food off easier, or square, which keeps slippery food on more firmly.

✔ Some metal skewers have a sliding block at one end to allow you to push the food down and off the blade.

✔ Metal skewers are an investment — you have to pay for them now, but you can use them for years to come!

✔ Decorative metal skewers can look quite dramatic on a platter.

✔ Bamboo or wooden skewers, which are usually sold and packaged by the dozens or hundreds, are significantly cheaper than metal ones.

✔ Because of the material they're made of, wooden skewers must be soaked in water for at least 30 minutes before using, lest they burn up. Wrapping the tips in aluminum foil also works.

Even after you soak wooden skewers in water, the ends of the skewers tend to burn anyway. Be careful when you transfer them to a plate.

Grilling Up Kebabs

Here are some pointers for skewer or kebab cooking:

✔ Pack the pieces of meat tightly on the skewer if you want the meat cooked rare or medium-rare. If you want it medium to well-done, pack the cubes or strips more loosely with a little space between each piece, allowing more heat to circulate.

✔ Cut the cubes of food into pieces that are uniform in size to ensure even cooking. A 1-inch beef cube grills to medium in about 10 minutes.

✔ Any firm-fleshed fish can easily be cut into kebabs about 1-inch thick. You want all the pieces of food on the skewer to be done in the same amount of time. Turn and brush fish kebabs frequently with a basting sauce, marinade, or herb butter to keep them from drying out. One-inch pieces of fish take 6 to 8 minutes to cook through.

✔ When serving an entire meal of grilled meat and vegetable kebabs, you may want to grill each separately. True, it looks prettier and is more convenient to grill the entire meal on one skewer, but packing these foods alternately onto the same skewer gives you less control and may result in food that is unevenly cooked.

✔ Be sure that round-shaped vegetables, like mushrooms or slices of zucchini and yellow squash, lie flat, with their widest surface exposed to the heat of the grill. Pierce them from edge to edge, rather than through their centers. (See Figure 5-1.)

✔ Foods such as cherry tomatoes or shrimp have a tendency to spin around as the skewer is turned. Try piercing these items with two parallel skewers, rather than one, to hold them in place, as shown in Figure 5-1. Or use square rather than round metal skewers.

✔ For pretty appetizers, cut your ingredients into small cubes or chunks of 1 inch or less and thread foods onto 6-inch skewers.

Figure 5-1: Various ways to skewer vegetables.

Use caution when turning your kebabs and always wear an insulated mitt. (Refer to Chapter 2.) The skewer handles get hot enough to sear the tips of your fingers.

Western Beef Kebabs with Red Peppers and Onions

In this recipe, you save the marinade that soaks the raw food and boil it to make a delicious finishing sauce for the grilled food. This particular marinade combines many ingredients common to American Southwestern cooking — lime juice, grated lime peel, garlic, jalapeño peppers, and ground cumin. A touch of butter is added, just as the sauce is reheated, to blend together the various flavors.

Preparation time: 25 minutes

Marinating time: 6 hours or overnight

Grilling time: 10 to 12 minutes

Yield: 4 servings

1½ to 2 pounds sirloin, or other tender beef such as top loin or round tip steak

2 medium red peppers

1 medium onion

½ cup apple juice, divided

6 tablespoons lime juice (about 3 large limes)

1½ teaspoons grated lime peel

6 tablespoons vegetable oil

3 cloves garlic, peeled and coarsely chopped

1 to 2 large jalapeño peppers, seeded and chopped

¾ teaspoon cumin

1½ teaspoons chili powder

½ teaspoon paprika

Salt and pepper to taste

2 tablespoons butter

1 Working on a cutting board, trim all visible fat from the beef; cut the meat into cubes of about 1½ inches. Place the cubes in a large, resealable plastic bag or other non-reactive container.

2 Core and seed the red peppers and slice them into strips about 1½ inches wide; slice each strip crosswise into 1- to 2-inch pieces. Cut the onion in half lengthwise and remove the skin. Cut each half into thirds; break them apart into slices. Place the peppers and onions in the bag or container with the beef cubes.

3 Combine 6 tablespoons of the apple juice with the lime juice, grated lime peel, oil, garlic, jalapeño peppers, cumin, chili powder, and paprika, in a blender container; whirl the mixture for a few seconds into a coarse puree. Pour the resulting marinade over the beef and vegetables; seal the bag or cover the container, and refrigerate for at least 6 hours or overnight, turning occasionally.

4 Remove the beef from the marinade. Reserve any remaining marinade and place in a small saucepan. Thread 3 to 4 beef cubes, alternating with pieces of pepper and onion, on skewers. (Soak wooden skewers in water for at least 30 minutes to prevent them from burning.) Sprinkle kebabs with salt and pepper.

5 Place the skewers on a well-oiled grill grid; grill the kebabs for about 10 minutes for medium-rare, or about 12 minutes for medium, turning every 5 to 6 minutes.

6 As the kebabs grill, bring the marinade in the saucepan to a boil over high heat on top of the stove; reduce heat and simmer for 1 minute. Whisk in 2 tablespoons butter and 2 tablespoons of the remaining apple juice. Spoon sauce over the grilled kebabs just before serving.

Go-With! *Serve with Grilled Potato Planks, or with Grilled Corn on the Cob (both in Chapter 8).*

Everybody likes their meat cooked to different degrees of doneness: One person's rare is another's medium-well. Always check the meat for doneness a few minutes before the end of the estimated cooking time by making a small cut with a sharp knife into the center of a few of the kebab cubes.

Threading pieces of food tightly together on skewers increases the overall cooking time. Leave a little space between each piece of food to allow the heat to surround and cook the food evenly and more quickly.

Lemony Fresh Lamb Kebabs

These lamb kebabs come to life with the flavors of fresh lemon juice, grated lemon peel, crushed garlic, and fresh rosemary. Lamb kebab cubes grill quickly, in only about 10 minutes. Be sure to hover over the kebabs, checking often for doneness, because they easily overcook and lose their juicy tenderness. They make terrific party appetizers.

Preparation time: *20 minutes*

Marinating time: *6 hours or overnight*

Grilling time: *10 minutes*

Yield: *4 servings*

6 tablespoons olive oil

Grated peel of 1 large lemon (about 2 teaspoons)

Juice of 1 large lemon (about 3 tablespoons)

1 tablespoon finely chopped fresh rosemary, or 1 teaspoon dried, crushed rosemary

2 large cloves garlic, peeled and minced

½ teaspoon salt, or to taste

Pepper to taste

2 pounds lamb (from the leg), cut into 1- to 1¼-inch cubes

8 to 10 long sprigs fresh rosemary (optional)

Oil for brushing rosemary sprigs

Lemon wedges for garnish

1 In a medium mixing bowl or large, resealable plastic bag, combine the olive oil, lemon peel, lemon juice, rosemary, garlic, and salt and pepper; add the lamb cubes, tossing to coat in the marinade. Cover the bowl or seal the bag, pressing out any air. Refrigerate for 6 hours or overnight.

2 Remove the lamb from the marinade, reserving any remaining marinade. Thread the lamb on skewers. (Be sure to presoak wooden skewers in water for 30 minutes to prevent them from burning.) Brush the lamb with the reserved marinade.

3 If using rosemary sprigs, brush them generously with oil. Place the sprigs on a lightly oiled grill grid. Set the lamb kebabs on the rosemary sprigs (or directly on the oiled grid, if you're not using the rosemary). Grill the kebabs for about 5 minutes; brush them with more marinade and turn. Grill for about 5 minutes more for medium-rare.

Cut to test: The lamb should be pink to rosy in the center of each kebab when done. Transfer immediately to a serving platter, garnished with lemon wedges.

Grilled Shrimp with Scallions in a Soy Marinade

These skewered extra-large or jumbo shrimp (16 to 20 per pound) are brushed with a sweet-sour glaze. To add a little contrasting color and crunch, wrap a long green scallion around and through each skewered shrimp. Or cut the scallions into 2-inch pieces and alternate them on the skewers with the shrimp.

Preparation time: 20 minutes

Marinating time: 30 minutes to 1 hour

Grilling time: 6 minutes

Yield: 4 servings

26 to 28 extra-large shrimp, shelled and deveined (about 1½ pounds)

6 tablespoons soy sauce

3 tablespoons sesame oil

3 tablespoons vegetable oil

3 tablespoons balsamic vinegar

2 tablespoons honey

3 cloves garlic, peeled and minced

1 tablespoon peeled and coarsely chopped fresh ginger root

1 to 2 teaspoons seeded, minced fresh hot chile pepper, such as jalapeño or habañero

8 scallions, trimmed (optional)

1 Rinse and drain the shrimp under cold running water.

2 In a medium mixing bowl or a large, resealable plastic bag, make the marinade by combining the remaining ingredients, except the scallions; add the shrimp to the marinade, tossing them to coat well. Cover the bowl or seal the bag, pressing out any air; refrigerate for about 30 minutes to 1 hour.

3 Arrange the shrimp, 3 to 4 to a skewer, on 8 skewers. (Be sure to presoak wooden skewers in water at least 30 minutes to prevent them from burning.) Pierce a scallion through its white bulb with the tip of a skewer (if desired), and then thread the long green part through and around the shrimp to hold in place. Repeat with remaining scallions and skewers. Brush the scallions and shrimp generously with the marinade, dabbing on bits and pieces of the chopped ginger and chiles.

4 Grill the kebabs on a lightly oiled grill grid about 3 minutes per side or until the shrimp are opaque and pink, brushing with the marinade once before turning.

Allowing fish to marinate longer than an hour, particularly when the mixture contains an acid like lemon juice or vinegar, can cause the fish flesh to begin to toughen. One way to strengthen the flavors of the marinade without risking this undesirable firming up is to chill the marinade in the refrigerator a few hours *before* adding the fish. When the fish is finally added, the marinade flavors are at their peak.

Chapter 6

Beef and Pork — Grilled Classics

In This Chapter

▶ Choosing cuts of beef and pork
▶ Grilling steaks to perfection
▶ Grilling pork chops

*B*eef and pork — thick, juicy, and full of flavor — are the quintessential grilled food. Whether you like your meat rare or well done, rubbed and marinated or plain, this chapter has tips and tricks for all your beef and pork grilling needs. We even help you shop for great cuts of meat.

Beef Is What Grills Were Made For

While this section is full of ideas for grilling beef, it isn't the only place you can find beef recipes in this book. For tips on grilling the perfect hamburger, turn to Chapter 4. For grilling a variety of beef kebabs, flip to Chapter 5. You can also find a large assortment of rubs, flavored oils, and compound butters — perfect for a variety of beef cuts — in Chapter 3.

But for tips on buying cuts of beef and grilling them to perfection, read on!

Hearty — and pretty healthy

Concerns over the high fat and cholesterol in beef, in our opinion, have been overemphasized by zealots who neglect to mention beef's healthful properties. True, a 16-ounce steak with baked potato and sour cream, onion rings, and a piece of cheesecake for dessert is not what you'd call a low-cal dinner, but it's not the beef that accounts for most of those calories.

Beef is an excellent source of protein, iron, zinc, niacin, phosphorus, and B vitamins. And both fat and cholesterol — in moderation — are essential to a human diet. A "portion," in today's definition, is a piece the size of a deck of cards.

Because beef, like other animal products, can carry all sorts of bacteria, follow these precautions:

✔ If the meat has been frozen, do not thaw it at room temperature. Bacteria can build up during the thawing process, and thawing in the refrigerator overnight makes for a better texture in the meat.

✔ Always store meat of any kind in the refrigerator or freezer after purchase.

✔ Cook all ground beef hamburgers to 160 degrees, with no trace of pink remaining in the center of the patty, and you will kill off bacteria that can cause food-borne illnesses.

You can cook other beef cuts to slightly lower internal temperatures.

✔ Never place the cooked or grilled meat on the same platter that held the raw meat.

The cut of your beef

Names of meat cuts can be confusing because there are regional and colloquial differences in the way butchers describe a particular cut. For instance, Midwesterners may refer to a luscious short loin without the fillet and bone as a New York strip, while people in New York call the exact same cut a Kansas City strip. Elsewhere it might be called a shell steak. London broil, often sold as a particular cut of beef, started out as a recipe made with flank steak. Today the term London broil is often used to identify beef top round, beef chuck shoulder steak, or flank steak.

When shopping for cuts most suitable for grilling, here's what you'll find at your supermarket (see Figure 6-1):

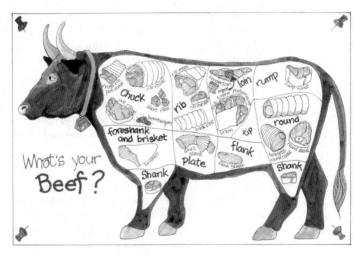

Figure 6-1: The cut of your beef.

✔ **Top loin (strip) steak.** The classic beef steak — also known as Kansas City strip, New York strip, and club. The top loin or strip steak is considered by many steak lovers to be the single finest cut because of its rich marbling, perfect texture (which is neither too firm nor too mushy), and its real beefy flavor. Strip steaks are usually sold boneless, although the bone provides an added succulence to the finished product.

✔ **Tenderloin.** A rather long, boneless piece of meat with three sections. The middle is called the center section, the larger thicker end is called the butt, and the tapered end is the tip. The whole tenderloin weighs about 4 to 6 pounds, but can be cut and bought as a smaller roast, as individual steaks, or as tenderloin tips that are good for kebabs.

✔ **Filet mignon.** A term for steaks cut from the small end of the tenderloin — the most tender beef cut available. These steaks cook quickly and are best if cut between 1 and 2 inches thick. A 1-inch-thick filet takes about 13 to 15 minutes for medium-rare to medium.

✔ **T-bone and porterhouse steaks.** Cut from the short loin section of the animal, these two are basically the same. Each of these steaks has two muscles — the tenderloin and the top loin (also called the *strip*). The distinctive T-bone (a bone down the middle of the steak that's shaped like the letter "T") helps identify each of these steaks. The difference between them is the size of their tenderloin muscles: The porterhouse has a tenderloin muscle about the width of a silver dollar or bigger, while the T-bone's tenderloin muscle is smaller than a silver dollar. The porterhouse is also called a *sweetheart steak,* because it's really two steaks in one and big enough for two servings.

✔ **Ribeye.** Boneless cut from the rib section. Ask for ribeye steaks from the *small end,* which is farthest from the chuck and closest to the more tender loin. The small end also has less fat, which is better for grilling. Cut them about 1-inch thick and grill over medium heat for about 11 to 14 minutes. If sold with the bone, these steaks are called *rib steaks,* and cook in less time, about 9 to 12 minutes for 1-inch thick.

✔ **Sirloin.** Situated next to the round and actually cut from the loin or hip portion of the animal, most sirloin steaks are sold boneless. They are fairly economical, tender, and versatile — they make great cubes for kebabs or strips for stir-frying. A 1-inch-thick sirloin takes about 15 to 17 minutes to grill to medium.

✔ **Flank.** Although considered less tender than the other cuts in this list, the flank steak has wonderful flavor when grilled and needs only a little marinating to soften. Cook only to medium-rare, carving across the grain into thin slices.

Preparing and grilling your steaks

Is the thickness of a good steak merely a matter of personal preference? Not to us. The best thickness for grilling any type of steak is 1 inch, although the most commonly sold steak in the supermarket is only ¾ inch. A steak that's 1-inch thick allows you more control than a thinner steak. A ¾-inch steak's degree of doneness can change in a heartbeat from medium-rare to medium on a medium-hot grill. So ask your butcher to cut your steaks 1-inch thick. You don't need to score the fat on a steak, but you may want to trim the fat, leaving it ⅛ to ¼-inch thick. A little fat makes the steak moist and juicy. Too much fat causes dangerous flare-ups.

Always thoroughly wash and dry your utensils and cutting surfaces after handling any form of beef (and chicken, too!). Also make sure that you wash your hands just as thoroughly.

Love them tender

Some beef is tender — some, not. Tender beef steaks, such as sirloin, porterhouse, T-bone, ribeye, and tenderloin, don't require marinating to break down or soften the exterior surface of their tissues. These cuts can be simply rubbed with combinations of seasonings that flavor the exterior of the meat as it grills. Use the rub and flavored oil recipes in Chapter 3, create your own rub from your spice rack, or check out your supermarket spice section for the commercial rubs suitable for beef.

Checking for doneness

Doneness is a matter of taste, but remember that even the finest prime beef has little taste or texture left if you cook it beyond medium. The National Cattlemen's Beef Association defines the approximate degree of doneness in beef as the following:

✔ Very rare: 130 degrees

✔ Rare: 140 degrees

✔ Medium-rare: 145 degrees

✔ Medium: 160 degrees

✔ Well-done: 170 degrees

✔ Very well-done: 180 degrees

These temperature guidelines are helpful when you're using a meat thermometer to take the guesswork out of cooking large roasts, but for steaks and smaller cuts, doneness is defined by the meat's interior color. Rare meat is bright red and juicy. Medium meat has a light pink center with light brown edges. Well-done meat is brown-gray throughout.

Less-tender and less-expensive cuts — flank, skirt, top round, eye round, and chuck steaks — need a longer marinating time. Marinate less-tender cuts in the refrigerator for at least 6 hours, or even overnight. Marinating adds flavor and helps to soften their tougher muscle tissues. When marinated and then grilled to medium-rare, these cuts can be quite juicy and delicious.

Within the categories of round and chuck, some cuts are tougher than others. Top blade and chuck eye (very tender cuts though they come from the chuck) don't need to be marinated longer than 6 hours. However, other chuck and top round steaks benefit from long marinating — 6 hours or overnight.

If you intend to use a marinade as a basting or dipping sauce, pour off and reserve a small portion *before* adding the raw, uncooked meat. Otherwise, any marinade that has previously come in contact with raw meat, fish, or poultry must be brought to a full rolling boil and then simmered a few more minutes before it can be used as a finishing sauce.

Grilling 'em up!

Usually, you don't need to *sear* a steak — that is, cook the steak for a few minutes over very high heat until well browned on both sides — as the initial step in the cooking process. However, bigger pieces of meat, like a thick roast or a 2-inch-thick steak may benefit from searing first, followed by cooking slowly over lower heat. For these bigger cuts, sear them, but not enough to blacken the exterior.

We are squarely in the camp of those who insist that allowing grilled meat to stand a few minutes before carving makes for a better steak. The juices inside will stabilize and redistribute throughout the meat.

Grilled Steak 101

Compared to the more expensive ribeye or porterhouse, a sirloin steak gives you lots of flavor for the money, and more versatility, too, because it's also perfect for cutting into kebab cubes. (Refer to Chapter 5 for Western Beef Kebabs with Red Peppers and Onions.)

This recipe features the flavor of a simply grilled sirloin and relies on only a little garlic, olive oil, and salt and pepper as seasoning. However, if you care to embellish a little, turn to Chapter 3 for an assortment of flavored oils, seasoned rubs, sauces, and compound butter recipes.

Preparation time: *5 minutes*

Grilling time: *15 minutes*

Yield: *4 servings*

2 tablespoons olive oil	2 boneless sirloin beef steaks, cut 1-inch thick (about 2 pounds total)
1 clove garlic, crushed	Salt and pepper to taste

1 In a small bowl, combine the olive oil and garlic. Generously rub or brush the flavored oil on both sides of the steaks. Sprinkle the steaks lightly with salt and pepper.

2 Place the steaks on a well-oiled grill grid. Grill 14 to 16 minutes for medium-rare to medium doneness, turning every 5 minutes.

3 Remove the steaks from the grill; cover loosely with foil and let the steaks rest for a few minutes before thinly slicing across the grain. Season with salt and additional pepper (if desired) before serving.

Go-With! *Serve with the Pesto Sauce or Tomato Chutney in Chapter 3, or with any of the compound butters in Chapter 3.*

Vary It! *You can substitute porterhouse steaks, cut 1-inch thick, totaling about 2 pounds, for the sirloin steaks.*

Texas Beef Barbecue

This marinade uses beer, lots of chili powder, cumin, and red pepper flakes to give an inexpensive piece of top round an authentic home-town barbecue flavor.

Preparation time: *10 minutes*

Marinating time: *3 hours or overnight*

Grilling time: *14 minutes for medium-rare*

Yield: *4 servings*

1 cup bottled chili sauce	1 teaspoon ground cumin
½ cup beer	½ teaspoon dried red pepper flakes
⅓ cup vegetable oil	1 boneless beef top round steak, cut 1-inch thick (about 1½ to 2 pounds)
¼ cup finely chopped green onion (white and green parts)	Salt to taste (optional)
3 tablespoons chili powder	

1 In a medium bowl, make the marinade by combining all the ingredients except the steak.

2 Place the steak in a glass baking dish or a large, resealable plastic bag. Pour the marinade over the steak, turning to coat. Cover the dish or seal the bag, pressing out as much air as possible. Refrigerate 3 hours or overnight.

3 Remove the steak from the marinade, shaking off any excess. Discard the marinade. If desired, sprinkle the steak with salt. Place the steak on a well-oiled grill grid and grill 12 to 14 minutes for medium-rare or about 15 minutes for medium, turning every 5 to 6 minutes.

4 Transfer the steak to a cutting board and let stand for 5 minutes, loosely covered with foil. Thinly slice across the grain.

Vary It! *You can substitute 1½ to 2 pounds of flank steak for the steak in this recipe.*

Cook any type of beefsteak according to your personal preference, but remember that overcooking tightens and toughens
muscle. The more a steak is cooked, the less juicy it becomes.
Cooking to medium-rare or medium gives you the most tender
steaks.

Pork — the King of Barbecue

Today's pork is among the most savory and healthful of meats
and is a classic grilled favorite. However, many cooks mistreat
that beautiful piece of pork and cook it into a dried-out, gray
wad — which in the past, too many people thought was the
correct way to cook it!

Hit me with your best cut (of pork)

The main thing to look for in a cut of pork is a firm, finely-
grained meat. Check to see that the lean part of the meat has
a healthy pink color and that the fat is firm and white, not
yellow. By the way, the iridescence that you sometimes see on
the surface of pork is perfectly natural — it's a reflection of
light off the cut ends of muscle fibers — and in no way affects
the flavor of the pork.

You can find a dizzying array of cuts produced by the meat
industry, though only a few — usually the choicest parts —
show up at the butcher shop or supermarket. (See Figure 6-2.)

The skinny on pork

Many people avoid eating pork
because they think it's a fatty meat,
and if they're talking hot dogs and
sausages (covered in Chapter 4) or
spareribs, they're right. But pork taken
from the loin and leg is not particularly
fatty. And for those concerned about
cholesterol, here's some good news:
According to the National Pork
Council, a 3-ounce serving of pork
actually contains less cholesterol than
beef or lamb.

Figure 6-2: The numerous parts and cuts of pork.

Here's the (pork) rub

Grilled foods don't produce the drippings that you get when you cook on the stove or in the oven. When you sauté, pan-fry, roast, or bake foods, the pan drippings (the browned bits left in the cooking pan) provide you with the start of an exquisite sauce to add flavor to your foods. But when you grill, the raw sauce materials drip, splatter, and waste away. That's why marinades and rubs (covered more thoroughly in Chapter 3) are used to impart flavor to grilled foods.

A number of international spice and seasoning combinations work well with pork:

- ✔ **French Provençal Rub:** Combine dried, crushed herbs like rosemary, thyme, bay leaves, salt, and black pepper.

- ✔ **Asian Spice Rub:** Combine anise seeds, cinnamon, ground cloves, ground ginger, and red pepper flakes.

- ✔ **West Indian and Jamaican Rub:** These have a lot of *heat*, or spice, usually in the form of cayenne, paprika, and hot peppers blended with the sweet complementary tastes of allspice, cinnamon, ginger, and dark brown sugar.

- ✔ **Greek-style Rub:** Make a marinade of olive oil, fresh lemon juice, oregano, garlic, salt, and pepper.

Cooking with rubs is beneficial because:

- ✔ **You can add rubs at the last minute.** Although it's best to give a rub at least 30 minutes to penetrate and flavor the food, if you don't have the luxury of time, you can still get good results — unlike marinades, which sometimes need hours to penetrate the meat.

- ✔ **Rubs usually contain little or no oil and therefore little fat.** Flare-ups on the grill are eliminated.

- ✔ **Rubs stick to the surface of foods better than marinades.** They form a tasty crusty exterior that complements the food's interior flavors.

And this little pork was done just right

Grilling pork can be tricky business, and it takes some practice to get it just right. Our grandmothers used to cook pork to an internal temperature of 185 degrees, believing that to cook it less would subject us to trichinosis. But we now know that trichinae are killed at 135 degrees. So, cooking pork to 155 degrees or 160 degrees is considered plenty safe and yields a much juicier piece of meat. One way to determine this, of course, is by using a meat thermometer (discussed in Chapter 2).

Furthermore, today's pork is bred leaner than the pork of our grandparents' day, with far less fat. Overcooking pork to 185 degrees results in a tough, dry chop or roast. So hover over pork chops as they grill. Turn them if they're cooking too fast.

Depending on the thickness of the pork cut and the amount of fat, muscle, bone, and grain of the meat, the cooking time for pork can vary considerably. Final cooking time depends on the thickness of the meat, the heat of the grill, and the distance the grill grid is placed from the heat.

- ✔ As you near the end of the estimated cooking time, cut into the meat near the bone to determine doneness before pulling the meat off the grill.

✔ A nice thick pork chop is cooked when its juices run clear and the meat is no longer pink near the bone.

✔ Brush glazes or sauces that contain any sweet ingredients like sugar or honey during the last few minutes of grilling to keep the meat from burning.

If you insist on grilling your pork until it's well done — we hope just because you like it that way! — you may still see some red areas in the meat, especially near the outer edges. Not to worry: In braising, this color comes from naturally occurring nitrites and nitrates (not additives); in grilling, the presence of exhaust gases from your grill may cause this red color. It's all perfectly natural.

Grilling is one of the tastiest ways to cook pork chops, which are especially delicious marinated, rubbed, or glazed, or simply seasoned with a dusting of salt and pepper. Pork chops for the grill should be cut about 1-inch thick for best results, so that they develop a nice exterior crust without drying out. In any recipe that calls for a pork chop, you can use a chop with or without a bone — but we find a lot more flavor in a chop with its bone intact.

Caribbean Pork Chops

In this recipe, pineapple juice gives the meat and bones in these chops a taste and crispness that is reminiscent of slow-cooked pork ribs. Use this marinade for other cuts of pork, adding some cayenne pepper to spice it up, if you want.

Preparation time: *15 minutes*

Marinating time: *12 to 24 minutes*

Grilling time: *10 minutes*

Yield: *4 servings*

1 cup unsweetened pineapple juice

¼ cup honey

¼ cup cider vinegar

1 tablespoon peeled and coarsely chopped fresh ginger

2 cloves garlic, peeled

1 jalapeño pepper, seeded and coarsely chopped

¼ teaspoon ground allspice

4 loin pork chops, cut 1-inch thick (about 2 pounds total)

Salt and black pepper to taste

1 In a blender container, whirl all the ingredients, except the pork chops and the salt and pepper, for about 4 seconds, to make a coarse marinade.

2 Trim all but ¼ inch of fat from each chop. Place the chops in a resealable plastic bag or a shallow baking dish; pour the marinade over the chops and refrigerate them for 12 to 24 hours.

3 Prepare a medium-hot fire in a charcoal or gas grill.

4 Remove the chops from the marinade, shaking off most of the excess; discarding the marinade. Season the chops lightly with salt and pepper. Place the chops on a well-oiled grill grid and cook them, uncovered, for 5 to 6 minutes per side, turning once. Cut to determine doneness. The chops are done when the meat has a light pink blush and there's no sign of pink near the bone.

Vary It! *Just about any fruit-flavored sweet chutney, marmalade, or jam (such as plum, apple, pineapple, or orange) works as a quick glaze for pork chops. You can reduce its thickness and sweetness by mixing with a little water or lemon or lime juice.*

Apricot-Glazed Pork Chops

In this recipe, apricot jam is mixed with cider vinegar, soy sauce, fresh ginger, and cayenne pepper for a sweet and spicy glaze.

Thick sweet glazes, laced with honey, brown sugar, jams, molasses, and other sweeteners, all work well with chops and ribs. But remember, the sugar content means that the glaze must be applied only during the last 5 minutes of cooking; otherwise, the glaze may burn and you may taste char instead of chop.

Preparation time: *15 minutes*

Grilling time: *10 minutes*

Yield: *4 servings*

1 cup apricot jam	*¼ teaspoon cayenne pepper, or to taste*
3 tablespoons cider vinegar	
1 tablespoon plus 1 teaspoon soy sauce	*4 loin pork chops, cut 1-inch thick (about 2 pounds total)*
2 teaspoons grated fresh ginger	*Oil for brushing chops*
2 cloves garlic, peeled and minced	*Salt and pepper to taste*

1 In a small saucepan, combine the jam and the vinegar. Cook, stirring over low heat, until the jam melts. Stir in the soy sauce, ginger, garlic, and cayenne pepper. Remove from the heat and set the glaze aside.

2 Trim all but ¼ inch of fat from each pork chop. Brush the chops lightly with oil; sprinkle with salt and pepper.

3 Place the chops on a well-oiled grill grid. Grill the chops for 3 minutes on each side. Brush both sides generously with the glaze and grill for another 4 to 5 minutes or until done, turning once. Cut to determine doneness. The chops are cooked when the meat has a light pink blush and there's no sign of pink near the bone. Simmer the remaining glaze for 2 to 3 minutes and then drizzle over the grilled chops before serving (if desired).

Chapter 7

Fowl and Fin

In This Chapter

▶ Choosing cuts of chicken for the grill

▶ Finding the secrets of grilling chicken

▶ Choosing the freshest seafood

▶ Grilling fish and shellfish

C hicken and fish offer more than great taste when prepared on the grill — they can also provide a healthy, nutritious meal. In this chapter, we provide delicious ways to prepare chicken cuts — breasts, wings, and quarters — and various types of seafood — steaks, fillets, and shellfish.

Making Feathered Friends

Almost the whole world loves chicken, and for good reason: It can be used in so many recipes, it is a fairly inexpensive meat, and as far as we know, there are no religious taboos against it.

The mild flavor of chicken appeals to just about everyone but a strict vegan, and the meat of chicken adapts extremely well to marinades, rubs, and seasonings. When choosing chicken, keep in mind that legs and thighs are dark meat and they take a tad longer to cook on the grill. The white-meat breasts cook quickly and, if not watched carefully, can dry out.

Keep that chicken moving!

Chicken, especially with its skin on, can be *seared* — browned very quickly — and can then turn charcoal-black just as quickly, without the inside cooked at all. This is something you want to avoid. The key to grilling chicken is to keep turning the pieces and to move them to hotter or cooler spots on the grid when some pieces seem to be cooking faster than others. Follow these steps when grilling chicken pieces with bone and skin:

1. Thicker, dark-meat pieces, which include the thighs and legs, take longer to cook than white-meat pieces. Place these pieces on the grill first.

2. Add the other parts of the bird — the breast and wings — after about 10 minutes, or when the legs and thighs have browned on both sides.

3. Throughout the process, continually turn the pieces from side to side, or to hotter or cooler areas of the grid as necessary, making sure that none of them are cooking too fast or turning black.

4. If you use an instant-read thermometer (refer to Chapter 2) to check for doneness, the boneless, skinless breast meat should register 160 degrees, and bone-in breast and thigh meat should reach 170 degrees. To check for doneness without a thermometer, make a small cut into the thickest part of the chicken. The juices should run clear, and the meat should show no trace of pink.

Handle chicken with care

Although American poultry production is carefully monitored and the facilities comply with all government sanitary and safety guidelines, salmonella and other bacteria that can cause sickness in human beings may still be found in chicken. Fortunately, these bacteria are killed off if the chicken is cooked until the internal temperature reaches 160 degrees for boneless, skinless breasts and 170 degrees for bone-in breasts and leg quarters.

Here are a few guidelines for safe handling and preparation of chicken in your kitchen:

- ✔ Always keep poultry refrigerated, even when in a marinade, until it's ready for cooking.

✔ Always thaw frozen poultry in the refrigerator, never at room temperature. You can usually thaw a chicken this way overnight.

✔ If any part of the bird has an odd or "off" odor, discard the entire chicken.

✔ Before cooking the chicken, wash it, inside and out, with cold water and then pat it dry with paper towels. Discard the paper towels.

✔ Thoroughly wash your hands, the utensils, and the work surface when you're done.

Grilling chicken breasts

Chicken breasts offer plenty of interesting grilling options. They can be grilled with or without their skin and bones; seasoned with any number of alluring rubs, sauces, and marinades; and sliced into thin strips or thick cubes for sizzling kebabs.

Breast meat is juicier and more flavorful if the breast is grilled with the skin intact. However, the skin contains a lot of fat that can cause dangerous flare-ups. You may want to opt for skinless breasts or pull the skin off before grilling. We start this section with an easy skinless breast recipe that grills in about 10 quick minutes (another advantage of cooking without the skin and bone — it's so fast).

If you want dinner in a hurry and don't have time to assemble a marinade from scratch, substitute your favorite bottled vinaigrette or Italian salad dressing. Marinate 4 to 6 boneless, skinless breast halves for 20 to 30 minutes in about 1 cup of dressing, being sure to shake off the excess marinade before grilling, to avoid flare-ups.

When marinating any food, remember to use a non-reactive container — one made of plastic, glass, ceramic, or other non-metallic material. Certain metals, such as aluminum, react with acidic ingredients like lemon juice or vinegar, causing the food and marinade to discolor.

Jerk-Seasoned Chicken Breasts

The smoky heat of the grill, combined with spices common to Jamaican jerk seasoning — cinnamon, allspice, cayenne pepper, thyme, and jalapeño pepper — give these chicken breasts their splendid taste.

Preparation time: *15 minutes*

Marinating time: *6 hours or overnight*

Grilling time: *10 minutes*

Yield: *4 to 6 servings*

8 boneless, skinless chicken breast halves (about 2 to 3 pounds)

¼ cup vegetable oil

¼ cup orange juice

3 scallions, finely chopped (green and white parts)

4 medium cloves garlic, peeled and finely chopped

2 tablespoons lime juice

2 tablespoons soy sauce

1 small jalapeño pepper, seeded and finely chopped

1 teaspoon brown sugar, packed

½ teaspoon kosher salt, or to taste

½ teaspoon ground allspice

½ teaspoon dried leaf thyme

½ teaspoon cinnamon

¼ teaspoon cayenne pepper

¼ teaspoon nutmeg

1 Trim the breasts of any loose fat; rinse them under cold running water and pat dry with paper towels.

2 In a medium bowl, combine the remaining ingredients, beating with a fork or whisk to incorporate the spices into the oil and orange juice.

3 Place the breasts in a large, resealable plastic bag or shallow dish; pour the marinade over the breasts. Seal the bag, pressing out any air, or cover the dish; refrigerate 6 hours or overnight, turning occasionally to coat the breasts in the marinade.

4 Remove the chicken breasts from the marinade; discard the marinade. Place the chicken breasts on an oiled grill grid. Grill for 10 to 12 minutes or until done, turning every 4 to 5 minutes. To test for doneness, cut into the breasts; the meat should be white and moist, with no sign of pink.

Just wingin' it

Once discarded by many people as not worth eating, the chicken wing has become one of the most popular parts of the bird.

Spicy Chili Chicken Wings

In this recipe, the delicate meat of a chicken wing is nestled around fla-vorful bone and wrapped in succulent skin. Serve these finger-lickin' grilled wings as part of a light dinner or make up a big batch when you need inexpensive party appetizers for a hungry crowd.

Preparation time: *20 minutes*

Marinating time: *2 to 4 hours*

Grilling time: *10 to 15 minutes*

Yield: *4 main dish servings or 8 to 10 appetizer servings*

3 to 3½ pounds chicken wings (about 15 to 18 wings)	2 teaspoons ground coriander
3 tablespoons olive oil	2 teaspoons paprika
3 tablespoons fresh lime juice	1 teaspoon peeled and grated ginger
4 large cloves garlic, peeled and minced	1 teaspoon salt, or to taste
2 teaspoons ground cumin	½ teaspoon hot chili powder or cayenne pepper
	½ teaspoon cinnamon

1 Rinse the chicken wings under cold running water and pat dry with paper towels. Cut off the wing tips at the joints and discard the tips. (Or wrap and freeze the tips to use later to add flavor to canned or homemade soups and stocks.)

2 Combine all the remaining ingredients in a large, resealable plastic bag or mixing bowl, blending them well.

3 Add the chicken wings; toss well to coat the wings in the oil-spice mixture. Seal the bag, pressing out any air, or cover the bowl; refrig-erate for 2 to 4 hours.

4 Place the wings on a well-oiled grid. Grill for 10 to 15 minutes or until done, turning with tongs every 2 to 3 minutes to prevent burning and to ensure even cooking. To test for doneness, cut into the thickest part of the wing; the meat should be white, with no trace of pink, and the juices should run clear.

Chicken quarters — drawn and grilled

Choosing chicken quarters simplifies the grilling process because you have fewer pieces to watch and turn. And some grilling chefs believe that quartered pieces retain their moisture and succulence better than individual pieces of chicken. As a bonus, chicken quarters look so inviting on the plate and are especially good as a special occasion or company dish.

Grilled Chicken Quarters with Barbecue Sauce

This recipe calls for two easy steps — preparing the barbecue sauce and grilling the chicken quarters. We think that you'll like the way sweet, sour, and spicy flavors come together in this barbecue sauce. If you want to crank up the heat, add more Tabasco.

Preparation time: *25 minutes*

Grilling time: *25 to 30 minutes*

Yield: *4 servings*

Barbecue Sauce

1 cup ketchup

½ medium onion, peeled and finely chopped

3 tablespoons fresh lemon juice

3 tablespoons Worcestershire sauce

1 tablespoon olive oil

1 tablespoon molasses

1½ teaspoons cider vinegar

1 teaspoon Dijon-style mustard

1 clove garlic, peeled and minced

¾ teaspoon salt, or to taste

¾ teaspoon Tabasco sauce

¼ teaspoon dried thyme leaves

Combine all the ingredients in a medium saucepan; bring to a boil, lower the heat, and simmer for 10 minutes, stirring occasionally. The sauce can be kept, covered, in the refrigerator up to a week.

Grilled Chicken Quarters

1 whole chicken (about 3 to 3½ pounds), quartered

2 tablespoons olive oil

Salt and pepper to taste

1 Rinse the chicken under cold running water and pat dry with paper towels. Rub the chicken quarters with the oil, covering all surfaces; sprinkle all over with salt and pepper.

2 Place the chicken parts, skin side down, on a well-oiled grid, and grill for 15 minutes, turning every 4 to 5 minutes.

3 Baste the quarters thoroughly on both sides with the barbecue sauce. Continue grilling for another 7 to 10 minutes or until the chicken is done, turning every 3 to 4 minutes. Cut into the quarters to test for doneness; when cooked, the juices run clear, and the meat near the bone is no longer pink.

The Gill and the Grill

Seafood makes a delicious feast for the grill. In this section, we introduce you to some delectable — and some unusual — ways to prepare seafood.

The fish story

Grilling fish is a job that causes many cooks to feel like, well, a fish out of water. This fear of fish is not surprising. The flesh of fish is very delicate, so you can overcook fish on the grill before you realize what's happening. In this section, we give you tips on how to know when fish is properly cooked and how to avoid having it dry out.

Grilling imparts a terrific flavor to the flesh of fish. Beyond that, the health benefits of eating fish are clear, from its low fat content to the omega-3 fatty acids in fish oil that can lower your cholesterol.

Start with fresh fish

Fish taken fresh from the sea or rivers has a taste unlike anything else. And anyone disliking fish because it is, well, fishy, just hasn't tasted a truly fresh fish. A fish just out of water, properly dressed and scaled and then grilled, is one of the purest of all culinary pleasures, and anglers take justifiable pride in bringing home fish of this quality.

The French have a saying about fish: If a fish smells like fish, it's not fresh fish. When shopping for fresh fish, here are some guidelines:

- ✔ Let your nose — not your eye — guide you. The one foolproof way to tell if a fish is fresh is to put your nose right up to it, especially near the gills. If you get a strong whiff of fishiness, move on.

- ✔ Don't buy fish that is stacked up on *top* of ice. A good fish seller buries the fish in ice.

- ✔ When poorly handled, frozen fish invariably loses its fresh smell and flavor, emerging from the freezer with a mushy or mealy texture and more than a whiff of fishiness. However, flash-freezing the fish — at –60 degrees right onboard gigantic trawlers — can maintain the freshness of fish much better than catching a fish and letting it sit around on ice for a few days.

- ✔ If you buy or store frozen fish, the best place to thaw it is in the refrigerator. Let it defrost slowly — 24 hours is best — and when the fish has come to refrigerator temperature, look for a nice plump, shiny appearance. Never, ever refreeze fish.

- ✔ Visit your seafood market frequently and get to know the owner. Let it be known that you expect good quality and good service. Show that you're serious about getting the best quality, and the owner will deliver the goods.

Thick and easy: Fish steaks

If you feel a little uneasy about your ability to grill fish, you really should have no problem with thick cuts of fish, especially steaks and kebabs.

If the fish steaks are sliced too thin, they will dry out on the grill and are likely to fall apart. Have them cut from 1 to 1½ inches thick for best results. See the section "Be gentle with fillets" later in this chapter for tips on grilling thin fish fillets.

Timing is still important, but with fish steaks you can at least blink without worrying that your fish is going to overcook.

- ✔ Most 1-inch steaks cook in about 8 minutes and continue to cook a little more after they're removed from the grill. However, cooking times vary according to wind, air temperature, and the heat intensity of your grill.

- ✔ Check the interior of the fish for doneness a few minutes before you expect it to be done. Use a thin-bladed knife to peek between the layers of flesh. Generally, when the flesh is no longer translucent, but rather opaque, and the knife meets no resistance, the fish is cooked.

- ✔ Fish will continue to cook after it's removed from the grill — you may want to remove it a few seconds shy of its fully-cooked time.

Fish steaks need little adornment in the way of seasoning. You can marinate or simply brush them with a little oil and seasonings before grilling. Throughout this book, we recommend using a large, resealable plastic bag to marinate food. However, fish is best marinated in a shallow non-reactive baking dish. With its very delicate flesh, fish should lie secure and flat in the dish, the marinade swirling around it. Tossing fish into a plastic bag may cause tender fillets to fall apart into small, impossible-to-grill pieces. Exceptions to this rule are, of course, shrimp and scallops.

Don't overmarinate! Fish tissue starts to react to the acid in the marinade and will fall apart in an acid-based marinade. Thirty minutes is plenty of time to add sufficient flavor to most fish.

Grilled Fish Steaks with Avocado and Citrus Salsa

Lime juice, orange sections, cilantro, and avocado give these grilled fish steaks refreshing flavor.

Preparation time: *25 minutes*

Marinating time: *30 minutes*

Grilling time: *8 to 10 minutes*

Yield: *4 servings*

4 salmon, halibut, swordfish, or shark steaks, cut about 1-inch thick, 6 to 8 ounces each

¼ cup torn fresh cilantro or basil leaves

¼ cup olive oil

⅓ cup peeled and chopped red onion, divided

2 tablespoons fresh lime or lemon juice

Grated peel of half a lemon or lime (about 1 teaspoon)

Salt and pepper to taste

1 large clove garlic, peeled and minced (about 1 teaspoon) (optional)

1 firm, ripe avocado, peeled, pitted, and finely chopped

1 navel orange, peeled, sectioned, and finely chopped

1 small jalapeño pepper, seeded and finely chopped

1 Rinse fish steaks under cold running water; pat dry with paper towels. Place the steaks in a shallow, non-reactive baking dish, in a single layer.

2 In a blender container, combine the cilantro or basil, olive oil, 1 tablespoon of the red onion, the lime or lemon juice, grated lime or lemon peel, and salt and pepper. Whirl in the blender for a few seconds until the mixture is a coarse puree.

3 Remove 2½ tablespoons of the mixture and reserve for making the salsa. Add the garlic to the remaining marinade (if desired). Pour the marinade over the fish steaks in the dish, turning to coat well. Cover and refrigerate for about 30 minutes, turning once.

4 Prepare the Avocado and Citrus Salsa: In a medium mixing bowl, combine the avocado, orange, jalapeño pepper, remaining red onion, and reserved 2½ tablespoons marinade. Cover the salsa and refrigerate until ready to use.

5 Remove the fish from the marinade. Place the fish steaks on a well-oiled grill grid, allowing some of the marinade to cling to each steak. Grill for about 8 to 10 minutes, turning once with a wide metal spatula. To check for doneness, make a small incision in the center of the steak with the tip of a thin-bladed knife. The flesh should be opaque, not translucent, when done. Spoon some of the Avocado and Citrus Salsa over each steak.

Be gentle with fillets

Delicate whitefish fillets (like those from sole and flounder) are not the easiest cuts of fish to grill and need some special care. Grilling is a rough cooking method, so laying thin, skinless fillets directly on a grill grid may cause them to fall apart, as can excessive marinating. So follow these tips:

✔ Grill fillets on a perforated sheet of lightly oiled heavy-duty aluminum foil (simply puncture the foil with fork tines). The foil supports the fillets. However, be aware that you won't get that wonderful grilled, charred flavor when you use foil.

✔ Keep your grill grid clean. Fish can easily get stuck on the little particles of cooked food clinging to the rack.

✔ Coat the fish with a thin layer of oil before placing it on the grid. Be sure to gently shake off most of an oil-based marinade before placing fish on the grid to prevent flare-ups.

Always be sure to oil the grid when it's cold to prevent dangerous flare-ups.

✔ After initially placing fish on the grid, resist any immediate attempt to move it around or turn it over. Letting it sear a little makes turning the fish easier.

Spice-Rubbed Catfish Fillets with Basil Mayonnaise

In this recipe, a bread crumb batter helps to keep the tender catfish fillets from burning on the grill, and a fresh basil and Tabasco sauce mayonnaise makes the perfect, assertive complementary sauce.

Preparation time: *20 minutes*

Grilling time: *8 to 10 minutes*

Yield: *4 servings*

Basil Mayonnaise (see following recipe)

1½ pounds catfish fillets

⅓ cup buttermilk

¼ teaspoon Tabasco sauce, or to taste

½ cup fine dry bread crumbs

1 teaspoon grated lemon peel

1 teaspoon dried basil

½ teaspoon dried thyme, or ½ teaspoon ground cumin

Salt and pepper to taste

4 sprigs of basil (optional)

4 lemon wedges (optional)

1 Prepare Basil Mayonnaise. Cover and refrigerate until ready to serve.

2 Rinse the fillets under cold running water and pat dry with paper towels. Combine the buttermilk and Tabasco sauce in a shallow dish. Combine the bread crumbs, lemon peel, basil, thyme or cumin, and salt and pepper in a second shallow dish. Dip the catfish first in the buttermilk-Tabasco mixture and coat both sides lightly in the seasoned bread crumb mixture.

3 Place the fish on a well-oiled grid. Grill for about 4 to 5 minutes per side, turning once, until the fillets are opaque in the center and the crumb coating is lightly browned. To test for doneness, make a small incision with the tip of a sharp knife in the thickest part of each fillet. Catfish fillets vary, from ¼ to ¾ inches thick. Final cooking time depends on the thickness of the fillets.

4 Using a wide spatula, carefully transfer the fillets to individual plates. Top each with a generous dollop of Basil Mayonnaise. Garnish with a sprig of fresh basil and a lemon wedge (if desired).

Basil Mayonnaise

Yield: *About ½ cup*

½ cup mayonnaise

¼ cup packed fresh basil leaves

I teaspoon fresh lemon juice

½ teaspoon Tabasco sauce, or to taste

Puree all the ingredients in a blender container until smooth, stopping as necessary to scrape down the sides.

Vary It! For mouthwatering sandwiches, serve these fillets on slices of toasted sourdough or Italian bread with sprigs of tart, crisp watercress or arugula leaves. For a lowfat dish, you can forgo the Basil Mayonnaise and serve these fillets with a simple drizzle of fresh lemon juice. Or use reduced fat mayonnaise, or fat-free yogurt combined with reduced-fat mayonnaise, for fewer calories.

She grills shellfish by the seashore

Grilling shellfish may sound like an odd idea, but you may be surprised to find out how tasty shellfish can be when grilled.

Mollusks such as clams, mussels, and oysters can be grilled directly on the grill or wrapped first in heavy-duty aluminum foil. Try to keep the delicious juices in each mollusk from spilling out onto the grill. It helps to place them, with their cup side down, facing the grill. Or, better yet, place them in an aluminum pan and then on the grill. The pan catches any juices that may otherwise drip through the grid.

Grill only those clams, mussels, and oysters with tightly closed shells. Discard any with broken shells or those that do not close when tapped. And never store these live mollusks in water or a plastic bag because they will die and soon become toxic. Place them in a large bowl, uncovered, in the refrigerator and use within 24 hours of purchase.

Be careful not to overcook naturally tender shellfish. Remove oysters from the grill when they open slightly. Clams and mussels will pop wide open when they're done.

Soft-shell crabs also do well on the grill. These days, frozen soft-shell crabs are readily available year-round — and they're not bad — but the best fresh soft-shell crabs start to come in mid-May, and the season is over before the end of summer.

Grilled Soft-Shell Crabs

This grilled crab recipe is divine. Serve with grilled tomatoes (see Chapter 8 for tips on grilling vegetables).

Preparation time: *10 minutes*

Grilling time: *6 minutes*

Yield: *4 servings*

3 tablespoons butter	3 tablespoons finely chopped fresh basil, or 1 tablespoon dried basil
3 tablespoons olive oil	Salt and pepper to taste
Juice of half a lemon	Tabasco sauce to taste
Grated peel of half a lemon	8 soft-shell crabs, cleaned

1 Melt the butter in a small saucepan; add the olive oil, lemon juice, lemon peel, basil, and salt and pepper. If you like a hot, spicy flavor, add Tabasco sauce. Brush the crabs with most of the butter sauce, coating both sides.

2 Place the crabs on a lightly oiled grid. Turn and brush every 2 to 3 minutes with any remaining basting sauce. Cook for a total of 6 to 8 minutes. The crabs are cooked when they appear bright red and firm to the touch.

Shrimp is a classic grilled dish — especially in kebabs. (Refer to Chapter 5.) In the following recipe, however, we show you a unique way to prepare shrimp, stuffing them with pesto.

SHOPPING TIP Try not to buy shrimp that has already been shelled, deveined, and packaged. This shrimp will have lost some of its freshness. Practice deveining it yourself or have your fish handler devein fresh shrimp the same day you plan to grill it.

Pesto Shrimp in the Shell

Grilling shrimp in their shells helps to keep the flesh moist and tender. A little pesto sauce, found in Chapter 3, stuffed into the shell adds flavor and color. If you have a wire basket, place the pesto-stuffed shrimp in the basket so that you can turn them over all at once. Purchase shrimp that is sized about 16 to 20 per pound, and sold as either extra-large or jumbo.

Although a little messy, this dish makes a terrific party appetizer; be sure to hand out plenty of napkins. Set the bright pink grilled shrimp on a large serving platter and garnish with lemon wedges.

Preparation time: *30 minutes (less if you start with cleaned shrimp)*

Grilling time: *4 to 5 minutes*

Yield: *8 to 10 appetizer servings*

1½ pounds extra-large to jumbo shrimp (about 24 to 28 shrimp), dark vein removed with shell intact	*Juice of 1 lemon*
	Salt and pepper to taste
½ cup Pesto Sauce (recipe in Chapter 3)	*8 to 10 lemon wedges, for garnish*
	4 sprigs of fresh basil, for garnish

1 Rinse and drain the shrimp under cold running water.

2 Stuff about ¼ to ½ teaspoon pesto sauce into the vein cavity and between the shell and flesh of each shrimp. The shell holds the pesto stuffing in place as the shrimp grills.

3 Place the shrimp in a large, flat dish and drizzle the juice from the one lemon over them; season with salt and pepper. Cover and refrigerate 1 to 2 hours.

4 Place the shrimp on an oiled grid. Grill for 4 to 5 minutes or until the shrimp are pink and opaque, turning frequently. Be careful not to overcook, or they will become dry and rubbery. Before serving, peel and taste a shrimp; serve with additional salt and pepper (if desired) on a large platter garnished with lemon wedges and fresh basil.

Chapter 8

Not for Vegetarians Only

In This Chapter

▶ Eating your vegetables — the grilled way!

▶ Discovering the thrills of grilling fruit

▶ Introducing the best toast ever: bruschetta

▶ Experimenting with grilled open-face sandwiches

Think "grilling" and you won't necessarily think of vegetables, fruits, and breads — but oh, are you missing something if you haven't tried grilling these foods! In this chapter, you discover the vegetables and fruits that you can grill successfully — every time. From corn to summer squash, apples to nectarines, we cover the gamut here. We also help you discover how to make bruschetta and open-faced sandwiches — all on the grill.

Veggies Not Like Mom Used to Make

Maybe if your mother had *grilled* your vegetables when you were a kid, she wouldn't have had to bribe you to eat them. Grilled vegetables take on the wonderful smoky flavors of the grill while retaining their natural sweetness and crunch.

Boiling, on the other hand, robs vegetables of flavor and precious vitamins, while sautéing and deep frying can add unwanted fat and calories.

It's true that delicate veggies need tender loving care while grilling to keep them from charring, but the delicious end results are worth that little extra effort. Here are some quick tips for grilling vegetables:

✔ Be sure that your grilling surface is scraped completely clean so that vegetables don't take on the flavors of other foods. Oil the grill grid well to prevent vegetables from sticking.

✔ You can't slough off while grilling vegetables — vigilance is important because vegetables can burn quickly. A slight char is very pleasing, but blackened, dried-out vegetables taste horrible.

✔ A grill topper (refer to Chapter 2) is a terrific grilling gadget to keep veggies, especially onions, from falling through the grid. If you're grilling directly on the grid, cut all vegetables large enough so that they don't slip through. Peppers can be halved or quartered before grilling and then sliced into smaller strips after.

✔ To determine doneness, use the skewer test: The vegetable is cooked if it can be easily pierced with a skewer. However, some people prefer a very crisp, almost raw, finish to their vegetables.

You can save time by *parboiling* (boiling a few minutes to soften) thick, long-cooking vegetables like potatoes, hard-shell squash, and carrots before grilling, but they taste better if you take the time to grill them directly. Cut them into chunks or thin slices to shorten grilling time. Only vegetables with very thick, inedible skins need peeling.

Simple seasoning (and brief marinating) is best

By far the simplest way to grill vegetables is to give them a brushing of oil — olive, peanut, corn, and safflower oils are all recommended — and a sprinkling of salt and pepper to taste. Other possibilities include:

- ✔ Grated fresh ginger combined with grated lemon peel and garlic beautifully seasons mushrooms and thin slices of acorn or butternut squash.

- ✔ Tarragon is terrific with eggplant and summer squash.

- ✔ Hot chili powder or Tabasco sauce livens up potato planks or wedges, or small new potatoes.

- ✔ Chopped fresh garlic, olive oil, and basil (mixed together) are good with just about any grilled, smoke-infused vegetable.

Many vegetables benefit from a little marinating before grilling. However, unlike meat or poultry, vegetables quickly absorb the flavors of the marinade and require only about 30 minutes to 1 hour of soaking — in fact, any longer may make them soft and mushy. If you don't have time to marinate vegetables, skip this step altogether and simply brush them with a little oil. Then, after grilling, toss them in a lemon-herb vinaigrette, using a bottled dressing, if you like. (Refer to Chapter 3 for some marinade recipes.)

Tossing vegetables with oil and seasonings in a large bowl before grilling is easier than brushing pieces individually. But don't try this with onions; they will separate from rounds into rings that are almost impossible to grill. Olive oils or vegetable oils, with their relatively high smoking point, are the preferred choices for brushing on vegetables before grilling.

Many vegetables can be seasoned and wrapped in aluminum foil packets before grilling (see Figure 8-1). They steam in the packet, retaining color, moisture, and flavor. Be sure to pierce a few holes in the top of the packet so that the grill's smoke can penetrate and infuse the food with flavor. To make low-calorie vegetable packets, use canned broth, lemon juice, and fresh herbs as seasonings, omitting fats like butter and oil. Be sure to combine only those vegetables with the same cooking time. For example, don't mix snow peas with carrot pieces, unless the carrots are cut into thin julienne strips or parboiled until almost cooked through. Turn the packets occasionally to prevent the food inside from burning, especially if you are grilling the vegetables longer than 15 minutes.

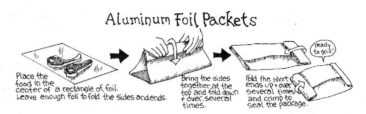

Aluminum Foil Packets

Place the food in the center of a rectangle of foil. Leave enough foil to fold the sides and ends.

Bring the sides together at the top and fold down + over several times.

Fold the short ends up + over several times and crimp to seal the package.

ready to grill!

Figure 8-1: Meat and vegetables benefit from aluminum foil packets.

Vegetables from A to T

In the following list, we give you tips for grilling a range of vegetables — from asparagus to tomatoes!

✔ **Asparagus.** Grilled asparagus develops a beautiful flavor and brown sheen. Trim off the woody ends and then peel the base to within 3 to 4 inches of the tip. Brush the stalks with oil that's flavored with a little crushed garlic and black pepper. Place the stalks perpendicular to the grill grid, turning so they brown on all sides. Pencil-thin stalks will be done in about 5 to 6 minutes, but thicker stalks can take up to 15 minutes. Stalks should be fork-tender before removing. Season with grated fresh pepper, kosher salt, and grated lemon peel.

✔ **Carrots.** Grilling carrots brings out their natural sweetness. Cut each into 2- to 3-inch pieces, brush with oil and grill for about 20 minutes, until tender, turning as necessary to brown on all sides. You also can first parboil in ½ to 1 inch of water for about 10 minutes; drain well and brush lightly with melted butter or oil before grilling for 10 to 15 minutes or until tender. Toss grilled carrots in a mixture of equal parts melted butter and brown sugar. Season with salt and pepper to taste. If desired, add a little Grand Marnier or other orange liqueur, or powdered ginger and crushed garlic. You can also wrap sliced carrots in heavy-duty foil with butter and seasonings and grill them (without parboiling first) until crisp-tender.

SHOPPING TIP

✔ **Corn.** When you're shopping for corn for the grill, always buy the freshest ears that you can find. As soon as corn is picked, its sugar begins to convert to starch, reducing its sweetness. Look for corn that is sold as fresh-picked or is at least kept cold to slow down the sugar-to-starch conversion. The green husks should look bright and fresh, and if pierced with a fingernail, the kernels should squirt out a milky-white liquid.

You can dress up melted butter for corn in endless ways. Add any of the following (to your taste) to melted butter for corn: lemon or lime juice, chili or curry powder, Tabasco sauce, cayenne pepper, soy sauce, minced garlic, finely minced dill, basil or cilantro, dry mustard, and ground ginger. For a butterless, fat-free, corn-eating experience, simply squeeze fresh lemon or lime juice over freshly grilled ears.

Grilled Corn on the Cob

Recipes for grilling corn often call for soaking the husks first in water for half an hour to prevent scorching as they grill. However, we find this extra step to be completely unnecessary.

Preparation time: 10 minutes for 6 ears

Grilling time: 20 minutes

6 ears fresh corn

6 tablespoons butter, melted

Salt and pepper to taste

1 Strip off 5 to 6 of the outer dark green corn husks.

2 Carefully peel back the remaining husks, leaving them attached at the base of the ear, and remove the silky threads.

3 Pull the husks back up and wrap them securely in place, using kitchen twine or a thin strip of husk.

4 Place the ears on an oiled grid and grill for 10 to 15 minutes, turning every 5 minutes. Peek beyond the husks at the kernels to determine doneness; the kernels should be golden yellow.

5 When the corn is cooked, remove the husks, brush the ears with melted butter (about 1 tablespoon per ear), and season with salt and pepper to taste.

6 Place the corn back on the grid (this time without the husks) and grill for 5 minutes more or until the corn is very lightly charred on all sides.

If you want the corn to be served with other grilled foods, you can grill it in stages. Grill the ears in their husks until the kernels are golden yellow and then remove the ears from the grill. About 5 to 10 minutes before the rest of the food is ready, brush each ear with the melted butter and place back on the grid — without the husks — to finish cooking.

✔ **Eggplant.** Some people say that eggplant is absolutely best when grilled, and boy, do we agree. Eggplant is a firm-textured vegetable that can be cut into large chunks for kebabs, sliced in half lengthwise, or sliced into rounds before grilling. Sautéing eggplant on the top of the stove requires a rich amount of high-calorie oil, but grilled eggplant needs only a thin coating of oil. Some controversy exists about whether the bitterness of eggplant is reduced by sprinkling cut slices with salt. If the eggplant is large, reduce the bitterness by sprinkling the cut rounds with salt and allowing them to drain for about 30 minutes. Before grilling, rinse the slices or wipe off the salt with paper towels. Smaller eggplants and Japanese-style eggplants have little bitterness and don't need this treatment.

To grill, cut eggplant into 1-inch-thick slices or cubes; brush with a flavored oil. (Refer to Chapter 3 for ideas.) Grill for 10 to 12 minutes, turning every 4 to 5 minutes until lightly browned on all sides. Toss grilled cubes into steaming pasta or mixed green salads or use them, along with sun-dried tomatoes and black olives, as a topping for pizza. Small grilled slices also can be wrapped around cubes of feta cheese or mozzarella cheese, secured with a toothpick into a roll, and served as an appetizer.

See the section "Sandwich face-off" for a recipe for Open-Faced Grilled Eggplant and Goat Cheese Sandwiches.

✔ **Garlic.** Much of the world is obsessed with the incomparable power of garlic when it comes to enhancing grilled foods. Garlic makes just about every grilled food, except perhaps those with sweet flavors, taste better. A whole head of garlic is a cinch to grill and has dozens of delicious uses. Mix it into mayonnaise-based dressings or rub it onto thin, toasted baguette slices with goat cheese and sun-dried tomatoes for a simple appetizer. Add garlic to salad dressings or to marinated vegetables or whip it with milk and butter into mashed potatoes.

To grill a whole head of garlic (see Figure 8-2), remove any outer, loose, papery leaves. Slice across the top of the head, removing about ¼ inch and exposing the ends of the cloves. Drizzle with a bit of olive oil and then wrap in foil. (If desired, tuck sprigs of fresh herbs such as rosemary or thyme between the cloves.) Grill for 45 minutes or until the cloves are soft and tender, turning occasionally. Squeeze out the roasted cloves. Individual cloves can also be oiled and grilled directly on the grid (without the foil) for 6 to 7 minutes per side or until tender.

How to Trim and Grill garlic

Trim one quarter off the top end of the head of garlic.

Pull off the papery, outside layer.

Wrap in foil and drizzle oil over the top and between the cloves.

After grilling, pull off the cloves and squeeze one end to pop out the insides easily.

Figure 8-2: Get great results with grilled garlic.

✔ **Mushrooms.** All mushrooms, whether cultivated or plucked from the wild, can be grilled. Mushrooms should never be soaked in water to clean them. Wipe off any sand or grit with a damp paper towel, or rinse quickly and pat thoroughly dry. Before grilling, slice off their stems so that they lie flat — very large mushrooms can be halved or quartered before grilling. Set mushrooms directly on the grid or skewer with pieces of fish, meat, or other vegetables. Baste them with an olive oil dressing before and during grilling. Grill about 5 minutes per side or until lightly browned. Overgrilling makes them dry and tough. Remove mushrooms from the grill when you can pierce their centers with a sharp knife or a skewer.

✔ **Onions.** Something about the taste of grilled onions is so appealing. Yellow, white, or red, onions have a natural sweetness that is released when they meet the heat of the grill. Yellow or red onions can be peeled and cut into ½-inch-thick rounds, quartered or halved. Brush the cut surface with any kind of marinade or dressing and grill. Depending on the thickness, rounds need to cook for 5 to 6 minutes per side. (Invariably, the rounds will separate into rings and fall through the grill grid.) Halves or quarters may take 12 to 15 minutes or more. Onion pieces are delicious skewered between pieces of beef, pork, or fish.

✔ **Peppers.** We can't heap enough praise on grilled peppers, which become transformed to a smoky-flavored, velvet-textured delight. Whether red, green, yellow, or orange, roasted peppers can be used in the following ways. Keep in mind that this list is just for starters:

- For a simple, elegant appetizer, wrap roasted pepper strips around whole balls of fresh mozzarella cheese; secure with a toothpick.

- Serve strips as a salad with a balsamic vinegar dressing, black olives, artichoke hearts, and cubes of mozzarella cheese.

- Toss strips into steaming pasta with creamy goat cheese, or grilled sausages, olive oil, garlic, and herbs.

- Place on any kind of beef, pork, fish, sausage, or vegetable sandwich.

- Place strips on toasted French bread with oil-packed sun-dried tomatoes, fresh garlic, and chopped basil for a hearty appetizer.

- Chop and combine with diced ripe tomatoes, black olives, and capers as a topping for grilled fish fillets and steaks.

- Puree into a smooth sauce and use as a colorful base for whitefish fillets or steaks. (Refer to Chapter 7.)

✔ **Potatoes.** All kinds of potatoes are appropriate for cooking on the grill. Scrub them without peeling, and then leave them whole or cut them into rounds, ovals, wedges, or chunks before grilling.

When grilling hard, woody vegetables or potatoes, use metal skewers to shorten cooking times — the metal heats up to quickly cook the inside of the vegetable.

Grilled Potato Planks

Sliced and grilled baking potatoes are a wonderful side dish for any type of grilled poultry, meat, or fish, and a healthy change from greasy French fries or pan-fried potatoes.

Preparation time: *15 minutes*

Marinating time: *30 minutes to 1 hour*

Grilling time: *15 minutes*

Yield: *4 servings*

4 medium potatoes (about 1½ pounds total), scrubbed	1 teaspoon dried marjoram, oregano, or dill
6 tablespoons extra-virgin olive oil	½ teaspoon Tabasco sauce, or to taste
1½ tablespoons white wine vinegar	½ teaspoon kosher salt, or table salt to taste
2 cloves garlic, peeled and finely minced	Pepper to taste

1 Cut the potatoes lengthwise into ⅛-inch-thick slices. Place the slices in a medium saucepan with enough lightly salted water to cover. Cover the pan and bring to a boil. Boil for 5 minutes or until nearly tender when pierced with the blade of a thin, sharp knife; drain thoroughly. Place the potatoes in a large, shallow baking dish.

2 Make the marinade by combining the remaining ingredients; pour the marinade over the warm potato slices, turning to coat. Cover and let stand for 30 minutes to 1 hour.

3 Prepare a medium hot fire in a charcoal or gas grill.

4 Before grilling, brush both sides of the potatoes with the marinade, being sure to include bits of garlic and herb. Place the potatoes on a lightly oiled grid, grill until lightly browned, for 6 to 8 minutes. Turn and grill until lightly browned and crisp on the second side, 6 to 8 minutes more. If desired, season before serving with additional salt and pepper, and Tabasco sauce.

Go-With! *These potatoes are delicious with steak, burgers, or pork, and ketchup makes a terrific dipping sauce.*

✔ **Squash.** Butternut, a pear-shaped squash with deep orange flesh, can be cut into rounds or cubes for kebabs. If you are in a hurry, parboil the slices, cubes, or halves with or without the skin; brush them with oil and grill for 15 minutes or until tender.

Summer squash, varieties like zucchini, yellow squash, crooknecks, and pattypans, are great candidates for the grill. They require no peeling and are delicious marinated, basted with a flavored oil, or even stuffed. Grilled rounds can be tossed into omelets, salads, or steaming pasta or served over couscous. Smaller vegetables are preferable because they have tender skin, few seeds, and fresh (some might even say sweet) flavor. Cut zucchini and yellow squash into rounds or cubes for kebabs, or slice lengthwise into ½-inch-thick strips. Grill for 10 to 12 minutes or until lightly browned on both sides.

✔ **Sweet potatoes.** Delicious, vitamin-A-packed sweet potatoes are also superior grilling food. They can be sliced lengthwise into long ovals or wedges, cut crosswise into thin rounds, or cubed and grilled on skewers. Brush thin slices or cubes lightly with oil that's flavored with garlic, and salt and pepper. Grill for 15 to 20 minutes until tender. To reduce the grilling time, cook pieces in boiling water until nearly tender, 6 to 8 minutes; then grill an equal amount of time until nicely browned.

Wrap whole sweet potatoes, individually, in heavy-duty or double-thickness aluminum foil. Pierce the foil several times with a fork and grill for 40 minutes until soft and tender. Serve with butter, a drizzle of maple syrup or honey, and salt and pepper to taste. Or complement the sweetness of the potato with a squeeze of lemon or lime juice and a pat of butter, forgoing the sweeteners.

✔ **Tomatoes.** Plentiful, ripe, and full of flavor in the summer, tomatoes are simple to grill. Red, round tomatoes — also known as *globe tomatoes* — are best when they're cored and sliced in half or into ½-inch-thick rounds. Then simply brush them with oil or butter that's flavored with garlic and chopped herbs. Grill them from 2 to 5 minutes, depending on thickness, turning once. Overcooking causes them to fall apart. Cook only until heated through and very lightly browned. Grilled tomatoes are a fine accompaniment to hamburgers, steaks, and any kind of chop or grilled fish.

Whole cherry and small plum or Roma tomatoes can be skewered and grilled until they're lightly browned and warmed through. Turn them often to keep them from charring and try to use square metal skewers to prevent the tomatoes from spinning uncontrollably when being turned. (Refer to Chapter 5 for more tips on skewering.) Combine grilled cherry tomatoes with chopped fresh basil and grated Parmesan or Romano cheese to make a delicious, impromptu sauce for steaming pasta.

Grilled Tomatoes with Cumin Butter

For an easy, complete meal, combine these grilled tomato slices with burgers, juicy steaks, fish steaks, or kebabs. Change the seasoning any way you wish, substituting other herbs and spices for the cumin. Or simply oil the tomato slices before grilling, and spread with softened goat cheese and chopped fresh basil after grilling.

Preparation time: *10 minutes*

Grilling time: *5 to 6 minutes*

Yield: *4 servings*

2½ tablespoons butter	Salt and pepper to taste
1 teaspoon ground cumin	2 large, firm ripe tomatoes, sliced about ¾-inch thick

1 Melt the butter in a small saucepan; remove from heat and stir in the cumin and salt and pepper.

2 Brush the tomato slices on one side with half of the cumin butter. Place them, brushed side down, on a well-oiled grid and grill for 2 to 3 minutes or until very lightly browned on one side.

3 Brush the tops of the tomatoes with the remaining cumin butter. Turn and grill for 2 to 3 minutes more or until very lightly browned, but not falling apart.

Grilled Fruit? Oh Yeah!

Grilling fruit takes a little more practice than grilling vegetables because the pulpiness of most fruits and the delicacy of their skin can be ruined by a grill that's too hot. Nevertheless, with a little care and imagination, most fruits come off the grill looking very luscious and toothsome — and they are definitely a surprise to most people at a party!

Here are some tips for grilling fruit:

- Allow the natural sugar in fruits (such as oranges and figs) to brown slightly when grilling, to bring out their rich, sweet flavors.

- Brush fruit slices, cubes, or halves with melted butter and brown sugar before grilling.

- Brush fruit with the same tangy lemon or balsamic vinegar marinade used for the main dish or salad and serve as a pretty plate garnish with savory grilled foods. Thick orange slices look especially attractive.

- Half-inch slices or chunks of apples, apricots, bananas, cantaloupe — yes, cantaloupe — papaya, peaches, plums, nectarines, pineapple, and pears take about 10 minutes to grill; turn frequently to keep them from burning.

Grilled fruits are enhanced by the bold flavors of brandy, rum, and fruit liqueurs. Impress your guests with this simple dessert. Skewer together assorted fruit chunks (such as slices of plums, nectarines, and peaches), brushed first with a little melted butter and brown sugar syrup; grill until lightly browned and bring to the table on a warm platter. Pour ¼ cup of warmed brandy, rum, or fruit liqueur over the fruit and ignite the dish. Serve with vanilla or rum raisin ice cream. Ice cream is the best companion to grilled fruits.

Foil-Wrapped Baked Apples

Here's an easy dessert that lets you complete most of the work before you get to the grill. Wrap the cored, nut-and-raisin-stuffed apples in sheets of aluminum foil and set them on the back of the grill behind other foods for your meal. If you plan it right, your baked apple dessert will be ready just as you finish the main course.

Be careful not to overcook these apples. Depending on the intensity of your grill's heat, they only need 20 to 25 minutes. Start testing their doneness with a skewer or the tines of a fork after 20 minutes and then every 5 minutes after that. They turn in an instant from cooked through — yet still shaped like an apple — to almost applesauce. Although the more done version is also delicious, it's not nearly as pretty.

Preparation time: *25 minutes*

Grilling time: *20 to 25 minutes*

Yield: *4 servings*

4 tart apples (such as Granny Smith or Macintosh), about 8 ounces each

¼ heaping cup chopped walnuts or pecans

¼ cup light brown sugar, packed

2 heaping tablespoons raisins

1 teaspoon cinnamon

¼ teaspoon ground allspice

2 tablespoons butter

2 tablespoons apple brandy or rum (optional)

Vanilla ice cream or sweetened whipped cream (optional)

1 Core the apples and place each on a buttered 9-inch square of heavy-duty aluminum foil.

2 In a medium mixing bowl, combine the walnuts or pecans, brown sugar, raisins, cinnamon, and allspice; divide the mixture equally among the apples, packing into their hollowed centers. Top each with a half tablespoon of butter. Fold up the edges of the foil around the apples to make a tight package.

3 Place the foil packages on the grid; grill for 20 to 25 minutes or until the apples are tender when pierced with a fork. (Be careful not to overcook.) Rotate occasionally to different spots on the grid to ensure even cooking. Remove from foil and (if desired) pour ½ tablespoon brandy or rum over the top of each. If desired, serve with vanilla ice cream or whipped cream sweetened with maple syrup or maple extract and sugar.

Grilled Pound Cake and Fruit with Brandy Sauce

This dessert brings together a heavenly combination of foods, sauces, and seasonings — grilled fruit and grilled pound cake, rum, brown sugar, orange peel, and vanilla ice cream. Slice the fruit as if you were preparing it for a pie filling; cut it first in half and then into slices about ½ to 1-inch thick.

Preparation time: *20 minutes*

Marinating time: *30 minutes*

Grilling time: *12 to 14 minutes*

Yield: *4 servings*

2 tablespoons butter	Pinch of salt
⅓ cup dark rum or fruit-flavored brandy	1 teaspoon grated orange peel
4 medium nectarines, sliced 1-inch thick	8 slices frozen pound cake, thawed and cut ½-inch thick
2 large ripe purple plums, sliced ½-inch thick	1 pint vanilla ice cream, or 2 cups sweetened whipped cream
3 tablespoons brown sugar, packed	

1 In a medium saucepan, melt the butter over very low heat. Add the dark rum or the brandy, the nectarines, and the plums. Sprinkle with the brown sugar and salt; toss to mix well. Cook, covered, over low heat, for 1 minute or just until heated through; remove from heat and sprinkle with the orange peel. Set aside for 30 minutes or longer. (You may prepare the fruit to this point and keep it covered until ready to grill.)

2 Remove the fruit slices from the sauce, reserving the sauce.

3 Grill the fruit slices on a lightly oiled grid, for 7 to 10 minutes or until lightly browned on all sides, turning twice.

4 After the fruit has cooked for 5 minutes, brush both sides of the pound cake slices with the reserved sauce; reserve the remaining sauce. Grill for 4 minutes or until the cake is lightly toasted on both sides, turning once.

5 Transfer the grilled pound cake slices to individual serving plates, two to a plate, and top with grilled fruit slices and a scoop of vanilla ice cream or whipped cream. Drizzle any remaining brandy sauce over the fruit, cake, and ice cream.

Grill to Go: Pizzas, Sandwiches, and Other Finger Foods

The idea of grilling sandwiches of any kind is of rather recent origin — which leads us to ask, "What took so long?" In this section, you discover how to prepare an easy alternative to pizza, called *bruschetta,* and how to make open-faced sandwiches — all on the grill.

Bring on the bruschetta

Bruschetta is a lighter variation of warm garlic bread. In its most basic form, bruschetta is a grilled slice of crusty Italian or French bread that's rubbed with fresh garlic and coated with a good-quality olive oil. But that's just the beginning. Italian cooks pile all kinds of toppings onto this tasty morsel, turning *bruschette* (the plural of bruschetta) into more of an open-faced sandwich or hearty snack. Toppings can include chopped fresh tomato and basil, or grilled eggplant and goat cheese, or grilled zucchini and grated Parmesan cheese.

Tomato Bruschetta

Here's a classic recipe that requires a minimum of grilling — only the bread slices feel the heat of the grill. You can make the chopped tomato topping ahead of serving time — in fact it's preferable to do so. This recipe makes a terrific appetizer.

Preparation time: *15 minutes*

Grilling time: *4 minutes*

Yield: *6 to 8 appetizer servings*

2 large red ripe tomatoes (about 1¼ pounds), cored, seeded, and diced

½ cup coarsely chopped fresh basil

2 tablespoons peeled and diced red onion (optional)

About ¼ cup extra-virgin olive oil, divided

1 clove garlic, peeled and minced

1 teaspoon balsamic or red wine vinegar

Salt and pepper to taste

12 slices crusty French bread, cut diagonally about ¾-inch thick

3 cloves garlic, peeled and halved

1 In a small bowl, combine the tomatoes, basil, red onion (if desired), 2 tablespoons of the olive oil, the minced garlic, vinegar, and salt and pepper. Cover and let stand at room temperature for at least 30 minutes but not longer than 2 hours.

2 Place the bread slices on an oiled grid. Grill for 4 to 5 minutes or until the bread is lightly toasted and golden on both sides, turning once.

3 Remove and immediately rub the edges and one side of each slice with a garlic clove half. (Use a half clove for every 2 slices.) Drizzle about ½ teaspoon of olive oil onto the garlic-rubbed side of each slice.

4 Stir the tomato mixture with a large spoon to thoroughly moisten; top each bread slice with about 1½ tablespoons of the tomato mixture. Place on a platter and serve immediately.

Vary It! *Here are some other ways to add flavor to bruschetta: Add chopped black olives or finely chopped prosciutto to the tomato mixture; omit the tomatoes and spread the bread with soft goat cheese or Gorgonzola cheese; or top with pesto or grated Parmesan cheese rather than the tomato mixture.*

Sandwich face off

When you eat a sandwich stuffed with your favorite foods, the experience can range from satisfying to heavenly. Grilling adds another dimension: Both the bread crust and the filling can be infused with smoky, grilled flavors. The sandwich recipe in this section is easy to make on a backyard grill or on a portable hibachi hauled out to the beach.

Open-Faced Grilled Eggplant and Goat Cheese Sandwiches

This healthy-hearty sandwich stacks layers of smoky grilled eggplant, tomatoes, goat cheese, fresh basil, and olives on French bread. Cut into small 3-inch pieces, to make lovely appetizers for a summer party.

Preparation time: *20 minutes*

Grilling time: *20 minutes*

Yield: *4 main dish servings or 8 to 10 appetizer servings*

2 small, long eggplants, about 1 pound each	Salt and pepper to taste
4 medium, ripe tomatoes (about 1 pound total)	2 teaspoons balsamic vinegar
	4 ounces fresh goat cheese, at room temperature
1 loaf French bread, about 24 inches long	2 tablespoons chopped fresh basil
½ cup olive oil, divided	Kalamata or other cured black olives (optional)
2 large cloves garlic, peeled and forced through a press or finely minced	

1 Cut off the eggplant ends. Lay one eggplant on a cutting board and, with a sharp knife, cut off a thin slice lengthwise. Repeat on the opposite side. Discard these slices (they are mostly peel). Slice the remaining eggplant lengthwise into ½-inch-thick slices. Repeat with the second eggplant. Core the tomatoes and slice crosswise into ½-inch-thick slices. Place the vegetable slices on a large baking sheet. Slice the French bread in half lengthwise and then in half again crosswise, making 4 slices, each about 12 inches long.

2 In a small bowl, combine 6 tablespoons of the olive oil and the garlic. Brush the cut sides of the French bread and both sides of the vegetables with the oil-garlic mixture. Sprinkle the vegetables with salt and pepper.

3 Combine the remaining 2 tablespoons olive oil with the balsamic vinegar; season with salt and pepper and set aside.

4 Place the eggplant on a lightly oiled grid and grill for 6 to 7 minutes per side or until tender and lightly browned. Grill the tomatoes until warmed through, 2 minutes per side. Place the French bread slices on the edges of the grid, cut side down; toast until golden brown, about 2 minutes; transfer, cut side up, to a serving platter or cutting board.

5 Spread the goat cheese on the toasted bread slices, dividing equally. Lay the eggplant and then the tomato on the bread slices, covering the bread completely; drizzle with the oil-vinegar dressing. Garnish with the chopped basil. Cut into main dish or appetizer servings. Serve with kalamata olives (if desired).

Vary It! *Substitute chopped, oil-packed sun-dried tomatoes for the kalamata olives.*

Index

Recipe Notes

_____

_____

_____

_____

_____

_____

_____

_____

_____

_____

_____

_____

_____

_____

_____

_____

_____

_____

_____

_____

Recipe Notes

_____

_____

_____

_____

_____

_____

_____

_____

_____

_____

_____

_____

_____

_____

_____

_____

_____

_____

_____

Ten (Or So) Ways to Make Grilling Healthy and Safe

Buy Meats, Poultry, and Seafood Last

Make the meat, poultry, and seafood sections of your supermarket the last place you visit before going to the checkout counter. Food can spoil in your cart while you shop for other items on your list. In hot weather, bring a cooler and some ice packs in your car and place meat, poultry, and seafood into the cooler for the ride home.

Shop Carefully

Check the sell-by dates on all products and look for mushiness, off colors, or strong smells. If you're the least bit in doubt about whether to buy a product, don't.

Thaw Foods in the Refrigerator

Don't thaw meat, poultry, or seafood on the countertop. By planning ahead (moving food for the next day's meal from the freezer to the fridge before you go to bed), you can cook with thoroughly defrosted food without letting it spoil. If you get into a time crunch, use your microwave to defrost foods. Microwaves are powerful, however, so keep a close eye on the food as it defrosts so that the food doesn't start to cook.

Marinate Foods in the Fridge

Marinating on the countertop is exactly like thawing on the countertop; both can expose you to spoiled food. Instead, marinate all foods in the refrigerator.

Don't Use Metal Pans to Marinate Food

All metal containers (except for stainless steel) react with the marinade and give a metallic flavor to marinated foods. Instead, use glass, ceramic, or plastic containers, which won't react with the acids in the marinades.

Avoid Reusing Your Marinade

Marinades pick up whatever bacteria may be on the foods you're grilling, so by pouring a marinade over cooked food, you could be pouring bacteria over food just before you eat it. If you must reuse marinade, boil it to kill whatever may be in there. A better bet, however, is to whip up a new batch for the pour-over.

Grill to the Proper Temperature

To kill bacteria that may linger in uncooked meat, poultry, and seafood, you must grill these foods to a certain temperature. Use a thermometer to check the temperature as your food grills. Don't insert the thermometer until the outside of the food is seared, or the thermometer itself could carry bacteria into the interior of the food.

Don't Cross-Contaminate

The bacteria that may be present in, say, your hamburger, can cross-contaminate your tomatoes if you put the raw burger and tomatoes on the same plate or touch the tomatoes after handling the raw meat. Keep cooked and uncooked foods completely separate.

Wash Everything in Soapy Water

Wash *everything* (hands, knives, cutting boards, countertops, faucet knobs) that may have touched raw meat, poultry, or seafood. We've heard stories recently of families handling raw hamburgers or chicken breasts, and then tearing up lettuce for a salad without washing their hands. The result? Entire families are sickened by the lettuce, which harbored bacteria that came from the food before it was cooked.

Wash your sponge by adding liquid detergent to it and squeezing the sponge until the suds disappear. Run your sponge through the dishwasher every few days and replace it every few weeks.

SPORTS, FITNESS, PARENTING, RELIGION & SPIRITUALITY

0-7645-5146-9   0-7645-5418-2

Also available:
- Adoption For Dummies
  0-7645-5488-3
- Basketball For Dummies
  0-7645-5248-1
- The Bible For Dummies
  0-7645-5296-1
- Buddhism For Dummies
  0-7645-5359-3
- Catholicism For Dummies
  0-7645-5391-7
- Hockey For Dummies
  0-7645-5228-7

- Judaism For Dummies
  0-7645-5299-6
- Martial Arts For Dummies
  0-7645-5358-5
- Pilates For Dummies
  0-7645-5397-6
- Religion For Dummies
  0-7645-5264-3
- Teaching Kids to Read
  For Dummies
  0-7645-4043-2
- Weight Training For Dummies
  0-7645-5168-X
- Yoga For Dummies
  0-7645-5117-5

TRAVEL

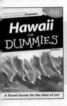

0-7645-5438-7   0-7645-5453-0

Also available:
- Alaska For Dummies
  0-7645-1761-9
- Arizona For Dummies
  0-7645-6938-4
- Cancún and the Yucatán
  For Dummies
  0-7645-2437-2
- Cruise Vacations For Dummies
  0-7645-6941-4
- Europe For Dummies
  0-7645-5456-5
- Ireland For Dummies
  0-7645-5455-7

- Las Vegas For Dummies
  0-7645-5448-4
- London For Dummies
  0-7645-4277-X
- New York City For Dummies
  0-7645-6945-7
- Paris For Dummies
  0-7645-5494-8
- RV Vacations For Dummies
  0-7645-5443-3
- Walt Disney World & Orlando
  For Dummies
  0-7645-6943-0

GRAPHICS, DESIGN & WEB DEVELOPMENT

0-7645-4345-8   0-7645-5589-8

Also available:
- Adobe Acrobat 6 PDF
  For Dummies
  0-7645-3760-1
- Building a Web Site For Dummies
  0-7645-7144-3
- Dreamweaver MX 2004
  For Dummies
  0-7645-4342-3
- FrontPage 2003 For Dummies
  0-7645-3882-9
- HTML 4 For Dummies
  0-7645-1995-6
- Illustrator cs For Dummies
  0-7645-4084-X

- Macromedia Flash MX 2004
  For Dummies
  0-7645-4358-X
- Photoshop 7 All-in-One Desk
  Reference For Dummies
  0-7645-1667-1
- Photoshop cs Timesaving
  Techniques For Dummies
  0-7645-6782-9
- PHP 5 For Dummies
  0-7645-4166-8
- PowerPoint 2003 For Dummies
  0-7645-3908-6
- QuarkXPress 6 For Dummies
  0-7645-2593-X

NETWORKING, SECURITY, PROGRAMMING & DATABASES

0-7645-6852-3   0-7645-5784-X

Also available:
- A+ Certification For Dummies
  0-7645-4187-0
- Access 2003 All-in-One Desk
  Reference For Dummies
  0-7645-3988-4
- Beginning Programming
  For Dummies
  0-7645-4997-9
- C For Dummies
  0-7645-7068-4
- Firewalls For Dummies
  0-7645-4048-3
- Home Networking For Dummies
  0-7645-42796

- Network Security For Dummies
  0-7645-1679-5
- Networking For Dummies
  0-7645-1677-9
- TCP/IP For Dummies
  0-7645-1760-0
- VBA For Dummies
  0-7645-3989-2
- Wireless All In-One Desk Reference
  For Dummies
  0-7645-7496-5
- Wireless Home Networking
  For Dummies
  0-7645-3910-8

The COMPANION GROUP